WITHDRAWN

Ancient Peoples and Places

MEDIEVAL CIVILIZATION IN GERMANY
800-1273

General Editor

DR GLYN DANIEL

ABOUT THE AUTHOR

Born in Vienna in 1926, Franz H. Bäuml settled in the United States in 1942 after spending three years in England. Following service with the U.S. Army during and after World War II, he took a B.S. in Economics, but then transferred to German Literature, taking his M.A. and Ph.D. at the University of California, Berkeley. Currently Professor of German Literature at the University of California, Los Angeles, he has contributed numerous articles to a variety of journals, and is author of Rhetorical Devices and Structure in the 'Ackermann aus Böhmen', *and of a diplomatic edition of the* Kudrun *manuscript.*

Ancient Peoples and Places

MEDIEVAL CIVILIZATION IN GERMANY
800-1273

Franz H. Bäuml

60 PHOTOGRAPHS
39 LINE DRAWINGS
14 MAPS

London
THAMES AND HUDSON

THIS IS VOLUME SIXTY-SEVEN IN THE SERIES
Ancient Peoples and Places
GENERAL EDITOR: DR GLYN DANIEL

DD
63
B14
1969b

First published 1969
© *Franz H. Bäuml 1969*
All rights reserved. No part of this publication
may be reproduced, stored in a retrieval system, or
transmitted, in any form or by any means, electronic,
mechanical, photocopying, recording or otherwise,
without the prior permission of the Publishers.
Filmset by Keyspools Ltd, Golborne, Lancs and
printed in Great Britain by Fletcher & Son Ltd, Norwich.
Not to be imported for sale into the U.S.A.
500 02065 5

CONTENTS

	LIST OF ILLUSTRATIONS	6
	PREFACE	13
	CHRONOLOGICAL TABLE	15
I	CAROLINGIAN CULTURE	23
II	THE SAXON AND SALIAN DYNASTIES AND THE AGE OF ROMANESQUE	44
III	THE CHIVALRIC PERIOD	88
IV	SOCIAL CHAOS AND CULTURAL CHANGE	147
	GENEALOGICAL TABLES	165
	NOTES ON THE TEXT	169
	BIBLIOGRAPHY	175
	Primary Sources	175
	Secondary Literature	177
	SOURCES OF ILLUSTRATIONS	184
	THE PLATES	185
	NOTES ON THE PLATES	217
	INDEX	223

ILLUSTRATIONS

PLATES
1. Charlemagne enthroned
2. Dedicatory page of Hrabanus Maurus' *De Laudibus Sanctae Crucis*
3. Elders of the Apocalypse, Codex Aureus from St Emmeram
4. Emperor Lothar
5. Initial from the Folchard Psalter
6. Initial from the Drogo Sacramentary
7. Ivory diptych
8. Auriga and Taurus, astronomical compilation
9. Imperial Chapel, Aachen cathedral
10. A page from the Utrecht Psalter
11. St Luke, Ada Gospels miniature
12. First page of the *Hildebrandslied*
13. Otto II
14. Book cover. Eleventh century
15. Goslar reconstruction
16. Goslar today
17. St Cyriacus, Gernrode
18. Henry IV at Canossa
19a. Bronze doors of St Michael's, Hildesheim
  b. The crime of Cain, detail of the doors
20. Reliquary. Eleventh century

PLATES
- 21 Bronze doors, Aachen cathedral
- 22–24 Pages from the Codex Egberti, Reichenau
- 25 Otto II or III
- 26 Nations of the Empire doing homage
- 27 Otto III
- 28 A page from the Codex Aureus of Echternach
- 29 Sacramentary, Fulda
- 30 A page from the Codex Aureus of Echternach
- 31 Book cover of the Bernward Gospel, Hildesheim
- 32 Ceiling of St Michael's, Hildesheim
- 33 Carved doors, Sta Maria im Kapitol, Cologne
- 34 Apostles and prophets, Bamberg cathedral
- 35 Nave, Speyer cathedral
- 36, 37 Pages from a Gospel, Abdinghof
- 38 Imperial crown, Vienna
- 39 Scene from a Life of St Gertrude, Hirsau
- 40 Page from a missal from St Michael's, Hildesheim
- 41 Birth of Christ, Salzburg
- 42 Synagoga, Hildegard of Bingen's *Liber Scivias*
- 43 St Paul and his correspondents, Halberstadt
- 44 Barbarossa as a crusader
- 45 Enamelled box. Swabian
- 46 Emperor Conradin, Manesse MS.
- 47 Margrave of Brandenburg, Manesse MS.
- 48 Walther von der Vogelweide, Manesse MS.
- 49 Ecclesia, from the *Hortus deliciarum* of Herrad of Landsperg
- 50 Archbishop Sifrid of Mainz with Henry Raspe and William of Holland, Mainz
- 51 Vaulting of the choir, Liebfrauenkirche, Trier

PLATES
52 Buttresses, Cologne cathedral
53 Nave, Cologne cathedral
54 St Quirin's, Neuss
55 Tympanum, south portal, Strassburg cathedral
56 Ecclesia, Strassburg cathedral
57 Synagoga, Strassburg cathedral
58 Bronze aquamanile
59 Chalice, Abbey of St Trudpert
60 Flabellum

FIGURES
1 *Map: The Empire of Charlemagne, p. 25*
2 *Signature of Charlemagne, p. 27*
3 *Map: The Christianization of Central Europe, p. 28*
4 *Map: Principal cultural centres, p. 29*
5 *King David, from the Psalterium Aureum of St Gallen, p. 32*
6 *A page from the Munich Heliant, p. 38*
7 *A page from the Munich MS. of Otfrid's Evangelienbuch, p. 39*
8 *A coin of the reign of Charlemagne, p. 41*
9 *Signature of Louis the German, p. 42*
10 *Signature of Otto I, p. 45*
11 *Map: Europe in the tenth and eleventh centuries, p. 47*
12 *Coin of the reign of Otto I, p. 48*
13 *Seal of Conrad II, p. 50*
14 *Map: Road network, tenth century, p. 51*
15 *Signature of Henry II, p. 53*
16 *Coin of the reign of Henry II, p. 53*
17 *Chain-mace, p. 54*

FIGURES

18　Map: Cluniac reform and the Cistercians in Central Europe, p. 57
19　Signature of Henry IV, p. 60
20　Coin of the reign of Henry IV, p. 61
21　Depiction of the battle on the Regen, p. 62
22　Seal of Henry IV, p. 63
23　Signature of Lothar of Saxony, p. 66
24　Romanesque capitals, pp. 68, 69
25　Miniature from the Codex Aureus of Echternach, p. 71
26　Missal of Henry II, p. 73
27　Map: Carolingian and Romanesque monuments in Germany, p. 75
28　Illustration from the Munich Passiones Apostolorum, p. 79
29　Depiction of human monsters in a twelfth century MS., p. 87
30　Seal of Duke Henry Jasomirgott of Austria, p. 93
31　Siege of a city at the time of the Hohenstaufen, pp. 94, 95
32　Map: Imperial palaces and castles in the Hohenstaufen period, p. 96
33　Map: The Hohenstaufen Empire, p. 97
34　Signature of Philip of Swabia, p. 100
35　Depiction of Saxon with Wendish prisoner, in the Sachsenspiegel, p. 104
36　Depiction of peasants and plough, in the Sachsenspiegel, p. 104
37　Depiction of peasants building a village, in the Sachsenspiegel, p. 105
38　Map: The spread of Gothic architecture on the European continent, p. 107

FIGURES

39 Map: The principal universities before 1500, p. 116
40 Depiction of a children's game, from the Annals of Genoa, p. 117
41, 42 Miniatures from a MS. of the Rolandslied, p. 118
43 Depiction of a accolade, p. 119
44 Depiction of a Hohenstaufen knight, from the Annals of Genoa, p. 120
45 Map: Principal representatives of pre-courtly and courtly literature, p. 121
46, 47 Miniatures from the Berlin MS. of the Eneit, p. 131
48 Map: Western and Central Europe from the eleventh to the end of the thirteenth century, p. 148
49 Miniature from the MS. 'Alexandri Minoritae Apocalypsis explicata', p. 149
50 Map: The Hanseatic League and other city leagues, p. 151
51 Silk, p. 155
52 Tomb of Rudolf of Habsburg, p. 157
53 Depiction of the Crucifixion of Christ in a Biblia pauperum, p. 160

For Carolyn, Mark and Deborah

Preface

IT IS THE BASIC premise of this book, that there were no 'German Middle Ages'. Medieval civilization in Germany—as in the rest of Europe with the exception of France—consisted of certain modifications of supra-national characteristics rather than of an appreciable number of cultural innovations. A mere account of these modifications and of cultural phenomena in general, however, is not sufficient for a coherent presentation of the most significant aspects of this complex subject-matter. Consequently, cultural phenomena are here presented not only in their German, but also in their medieval context, in order to place medieval civilization in Germany in cultural perspective. For the same reason, attention is frequently invited to analogous developments in different types of activity, such as architecture, literature, politics, and painting. Although some critics dispute the validity of such analogies, their pertinence is assured by the fact that the perception of phenomena is conditioned by culturally determined patterns, which form the common basis of the different idioms of artistic expression.

The author's translations of Middle High German poems make no pretence to poetic value. A poem cannot be translated: either the meaning of the original text is translated, or a compromise is sought between 'translating' the meaning of the text and all the other aspects of poetic expression, such as sound, rhythm, and semantic associations. The latter process may result in the creation, not the translation of a poem. The present purpose, however, is best served by the first alternative: a reasonably exact rendering of the meaning, rhyme-pattern, and metre of the original, so that the reader may receive an adequate impression of the Middle High German poem.

The epic and lyric poetry of the end of the twelfth and the beginning of the thirteenth century constitutes one of the two qualitative peaks in the history of German literature as a whole—the second such high-point is, of course, the Classicism of the Goethe period. Since, in addition, chivalric literature is the principal and almost the only source of our knowledge of 'courtly' civilization as a phenomenon in intellectual and social history, its extensive treatment in the third chapter appears not only justified but necessary. The analyses of some of these works—the best-known and most representative of the period—are meant to elucidate methods of coping with problems common to most of medieval literature.

I should like to express my thanks to Professor David Lang of the University of London, for first suggesting that I write this book; to Dr Glyn Daniel, for accepting the idea for the 'Ancient Peoples and Places' series, and to Mr Eric Peters of Thames and Hudson, Ltd., for shepherding author and manuscript through many a turnstile.

I owe a great debt of gratitude to Miss Edda Spielmann, from whose keen critical awareness, penchant for logic, and willingness to sacrifice her time, this book has benefited on every page; and to my wife, whose stylistic suggestions have eliminated many a fault and whose patience has made the writing of this book possible under most trying circumstances.

F.H.B.

Chronological Table

Some events in German history

481–511   Unification of the lands of the Salian and Ripuarian Franks under Clovis. Foundation of the realm of the Franks (Merovingian realm).

496   Defeat of the Alemanni. Clovis' acceptance of the Christian faith after his victory made the internal unity of conquerors and conquered possible.

510   Division of the Frankish realm among the sons of Clovis and continuation of the conquests.

534   Victory over the Thuringians and conquest of Burgundy.

550–751   Decadence of the Merovingian kings and their gradual replacement as sources of power by the mayors of the palace.

751   Pipin, mayor of the palace, crowned king of the Franks

Some events in general European history

493   Murder of Odoacer by Theodoric, recognition of the latter as ruler of Italy by the East Roman empire.

492–496   Pope Gelasius I. Origin of the medieval concept of the two powers, the spiritual and the secular, and the independence of the former.

529–534   Publication of the Codex Justinianus, the basis of the Roman law.

534   Destruction of the Vandal realm.

553   Destruction of the realm of the Ostrogoths.

590–604   Pope Gregory the Great.

673–735   The Venerable Bede.

c. 570–632   Mohammed.

664   Synod of Whitby.

711   Destruction of the Visigothic kingdom of Spain.

c. 725   Probable composition of *Beowulf*.

Medieval Civilization in Germany

	after dethronement of the last Merovingian.		
768–814	Charles the Great.		
772–804	Conquest and Christianization of the Saxons.		
c. 770	*Hildebrandslied.*		
774	Conquest of the Lombard kingdom.	778	Battle of Roncesvalles, death of Roland.
795	Extension of the Frankish realm to the Traisen, between Melk and Vienna, and Frankish suzerainty to the Danube and Save. Victory over Avars in Hungary.		
800	Charles crowned emperor.		
804	Imperial chapel consecrated at Aachen.		
814–840	Louis the Pious. Weakening of central power, wars between Louis' sons, incursions of Normans, Slavs, Saracens.	836	Vikings sack London.
c. 830	*Heliant.*		
842	Strassburg Oaths, alliance between Charles the Bald and Louis the German against Lothar.		
843	Treaty of Verdun, division of the Frankish empire: West Frankish realm under Charles the Bald, East Frankish realm under Louis the German, Middle Kingdom from the English Channel to Central Italy under Lothar, who received the imperial title.	845	Vikings sack Paris and Hamburg.
		849–899	King Alfred.

Chronological Table

863–871	Otfrid's *Evangelienbuch*.
870	Treaty of Mersen. Division of Middle Kingdom, from the North Sea to the Burgundian border, between Charles the Bald and Louis the German.
876–887	Charles (III) the Fat, son of Louis the German, briefly reunited Frankish realm (885–887).
887–899	Arnulf of Carinthia king of East Frankish realm.
900–911	Louis the Child, the last of the East Frankish Carolingians.
911–918	Conrad I, a Franconian, elected king by Franconians as well as Saxons, and recognized also by Bavarians. Designates duke of Saxony, Henry, as his successor.
919–936	Henry I.
928–929	Campaigns against the Slavs, conquest of Brandenburg.
933	Defeat of the Magyars at Riade on the Unstrut.
936–973	Otto (I) the Great.
939	Revolt of the dukes of Franconia, Bavaria, Lorraine, and Otto's brother

874	Settlement of Iceland.
860	Foundation of Novgorod.
865/6	Danelaw.
881–882	Vikings sack Cologne.
882	Conquest of Kiev.
900–940	Reconquest of the Danelaw. Edward the Elder and Athelstan of Wessex the first kings of all England.
910	Foundation of Cluny.
927–941	Reforming activities of Odo, abbot of Cluny.
937	Athelstan victorious at Brunanburgh.
c. 945–1003	Gerbert of Aurillac.

Medieval Civilization in Germany

	Henry, put down with the aid of Swabia.		
c. 950–1022	Notker Labeo.		
951	First journey of Otto to Italy, marriage with Adelheid, heiress of the Lombard realm (Italy). Otto king of the Lombards.		
955	Defeat of the Magyars on the Lechfeld near Augsburg. Defeat of the Slavs in Mecklenburg.	c. 955–c. 1020	Aelfric.
		959–975	King Edgar.
961	Second journey of Otto to Italy.		
962	Otto crowned emperor.		
968	Foundation of the archbishopric of Magdeburg.		
973–983	Otto II.	978–1016	King Ethelred II.
c. 980	Codex Egberti.	980–1036	Avicenna.
982	Defeat of imperial army by the Saracens near Cotrone in Calabria.		
983	Revolt of the Slavs and end of German domination east of the Elbe.	984	Eric the Red settles Greenland.
983–1002	Otto III.		
1002–1024	Henry II.	987	Foundation of the Capetian dynasty by Hugh Capet.
1024–1039	Conrad II, the first Salian king.		
c. 1030	Construction begun on Speyer cathedral.	1016	Canute chosen king of England.
1033	Accession of Burgundy to the empire.		
1039–1056	Henry III.	1054	Schism of Eastern and Western Churches.
1056–1106	Henry IV.		
1063	Strassburg version of the *Ezzolied*.	1066	Battle of Hastings.

Chronological Table

1075	Defeat of the Saxon rebels near Homburg on the Unstrut.	1070	Construction begun on Canterbury cathedral.
1076	Synod of Worms, deposition of Pope Gregory VII by Henry IV, excommunication and deposition of Henry IV by the Pope.	1075	Pope Gregory VII publishes the *Dictatus papae*.
1077	Henry's penance before the Pope at Canossa. Rudolf of Rheinfelden elected anti-king.	1077	First English Cluniac monastery founded at Lewes.
1080	Second and ineffectual excommunication of Henry.		
1084	Henry crowned emperor by anti-Pope.	1086	Domesday survey.
1085	*Annolied*.	1087	Death of William the Conqueror.
		1090–1153	Bernard of Clairvaux.
		1093–1109	Anselm archbishop of Canterbury.
		1096–1099	First Crusade.
		1099	Capture of Jerusalem.
1106–1125	Henry V.	c. 1100	Composition of *Song of Roland*.
1120	Vorau version of *Ezzolied*.	1115–1153	St Bernard abbot of Clairvaux.
1122	Concordat of Worms.	1121	Condemnation of Abelard at Soissons.
1125–1137	Lothar of Supplinburg, duke of Saxony, elected emperor rather than Frederick II of Swabia, a Hohenstaufen.		
		1130	Count Roger II crowned king of Sicily.
		1137	Geoffrey of Monmouth, *Historia regum Britanniae*.

Medieval Civilization in Germany

1140–1150	Lamprecht's *Alexander*.	1140	Condemnation of Abelard at Sens.
1137–1152	Conrad III of Hohenstaufen elected in preference to the Welf Henry the Proud, duke of Bavaria and Saxony; hence the rivalry between Welfs and Hohenstaufen.		
1147	Wendish crusade.	1147–1149	Second Crusade.
		1151	Death of abbot Suger of St Denis.
c. 1160	*König Rother*.		
1152–1190	Frederick I Barbarossa.		
		1155	Wace's *Roman de Brut*.
		1154–1189	Henry II, king of England.
1156	Creation of the duchy of Austria.		
1157	Diet of Besançon, conflict between emperor and Pope.		
1158	Diet of Roncaglia, assertion of royal powers over Italian cities; resistance of the latter.		
c. 1160	Der Kürenberger, Dietmar v. Aist.	1160–1170	Composition of the 'lais' of Marie de France.
1162	Destruction of Milan, League of Lombard cities against the emperor.	1163	Construction of Notre-Dame in Paris begun.
		1165–1190	Composition of Chrétien de Troyes' romances of chivalry.
c. 1170	Konrad's *Rolandslied*, Heinr. of Veldeke begins work on *Eneit*; birth of Walther von der Vogelweide.	1170	Murder of Thomas á Becket.
		c. 1170–1221	St Dominic, founder of Dominican order.
		c. 1174–1186	Composition of *De arte honeste amandi* by Andreas Capellanus.

Chronological Table

1177	Peace of Venice with the Pope.		
1180–1185	Composition of Hartman's *Erec*.	1180	Philip Augustus, king of France.
		c. 1181–1226	St Francis of Assisi, founder of Franciscan order.
1183	Peace of Constance with the Lombard cities.	1187	Conquest of Jerusalem by Sultan Saladin.
		1189–1192	Third Crusade.
1190–1197	Henry VI.		
		1193	King Richard Coeur-de-Lion surrendered to the emperor by duke Leopold of Austria.
1198	Double election: Philip of Swabia and Otto IV, son of Henry the Lion.	1199–1216	John, king of England.
c. 1200	*Nibelungenlied, Iwein,* Wolfram of Eschenbach begins *Parzival*.	c. 1200	Jean Bodel, *Jeu de St Nicholas*.
c. 1205	Death of Reinmar of Hagenau.	1207–1213	Geoffroi de Villehardouin, *Histoire de la Conquête de Constantinople*.
1208	Assassination of Philip of Swabia, recognition of Otto IV.	1209–1229	Albigensian wars.
c. 1210	Death of Gottfried of Strassburg.		
1212	Election of Frederick II.		
1214	Battle of Bouvines, defeat of Otto IV.	1215	Magna Carta.
1215–1250	Frederick II.		
1220	*Confederatio cum principibus ecclesiasticis*.		
1220–1225	Rudolf of Ems, *Der gute Gerhard*.	c. 1225	Composition of the prose *Lancelot, Aucassin et Nicolette*.

		1225–1240	Guillaume de Lorris, *Roman de la Rose*.
		1228	Frederick II conquers Jerusalem.
c. 1230	Death of Walther von der Vogelweide.		
1232	*Statutum in favorem principum*.		
c. 1250	Composition of *Kudrun*.		
1250–1254	Conrad IV.		
1266	Defeat and death of Manfred, son of Frederick II, at Benevento.		
1268	Execution of Conradin at Naples.		
1256–1273	Interregnum.		
1273	Election of Rudolf of Habsburg.	1274	Death of St Thomas Aquinas.

Chapter I

Carolingian Culture

IT IS CONVENIENT, and therefore customary, to begin a survey of German civilization as a whole, or its medieval phase, with the Carolingian era. Charlemagne's coronation in Rome on Christmas Day in the year 800 can be presented, by oversimplification, as the point of departure for the development of the medieval *sacrum imperium,* whose crown was worn with varying degrees of unease by the heads of German dynasties. Upon this basis the conflicts between emperor and pope, *sacrum imperium* and *sacerdotum,* can be presented as providing the pattern, directly or indirectly, for most other political developments in medieval Germany.[1] There is, of course, much to be said for this type of presentation; among other things, that it is essentially correct. However, it has two disadvantages: it tends to obscure the fact that—particularly in respect to those parts of the realm of Charles the Great which can be designated as German—few of the achievements which characterize Charles' reign survived the reigns of the later Carolingians or, indeed, his own. Secondly, it is a mistake to view these achievements as being in any sense monolithic. It is, of course, true that Charles created a centralized government, that he saw to the training of his governmental administrators at his own court, and that he took steps to standardize the administration of justice. But one glance at the map, and at the cultural conditions of the great variety of peoples within Charles' empire, makes it quite clear that anything like a monolithic political or social structure is simply unthinkable. Charles himself recognized the impossibility of carrying out rigidly consistent administrative policies: his *capitula missorum,* for instance, which contained instructions for his provincial inspectors, are an expression of the intent to centralize governmental administration. Of no less significance, however, were the

Plate 1

Fig. 1

capitularia legibus addenda, which furthered the development of the various tribal laws.

The social and cultural differences among the components of the empire of Charles increased in the course of its fragmentation, which began with its division into the parts to be ruled by the sons of Louis the Pious: Lothar, Louis the German, and Charles the Bald. In fact, the division of the realm by the Treaty of Verdun (843) had the effect of splitting the dynasty permanently and creating the basis for a German, as distinct from a French, cultural and political entity. Within each of these new realms the process of fragmentation continued over the succeeding generations of Carolingians. There is evidence that recognition was accorded the two separate entities, the French and the German, quite early, even a year before the Treaty of Verdun, in the trilingual (Old French, Old High German, and Latin) Strassburg Oaths, by which Louis the German and Charles the Bald swore mutual fealty.

The admixture of the monolithic and disparate, of the imperial—conceived of throughout the Middle Ages as direct continuation of the Roman Empire—and the tribal, of the Christian and the Germanic pagan, is reflected in the arts of the period.

During the interval between the Roman domination of Gaul and south-central Europe and the reign of Charlemagne, artistic and scholarly activity in that part of the continent all but ceased. Scholarship was confined to a few episcopal courts, such as that of Gregory of Tours, where there was relative safety from incessant social upheavals; artists concentrated on the ornamentation of small, and therefore portable, trinkets and objects of utility. Increased stability, both social and political, which was the result of the endeavour of Charlemagne to centralize his government, together with the need for trained administrators, provided the conditions under which learning and the arts could receive a renewed impetus. To a large extent this impetus emanated from the person of Charles himself, who, according to his biographer

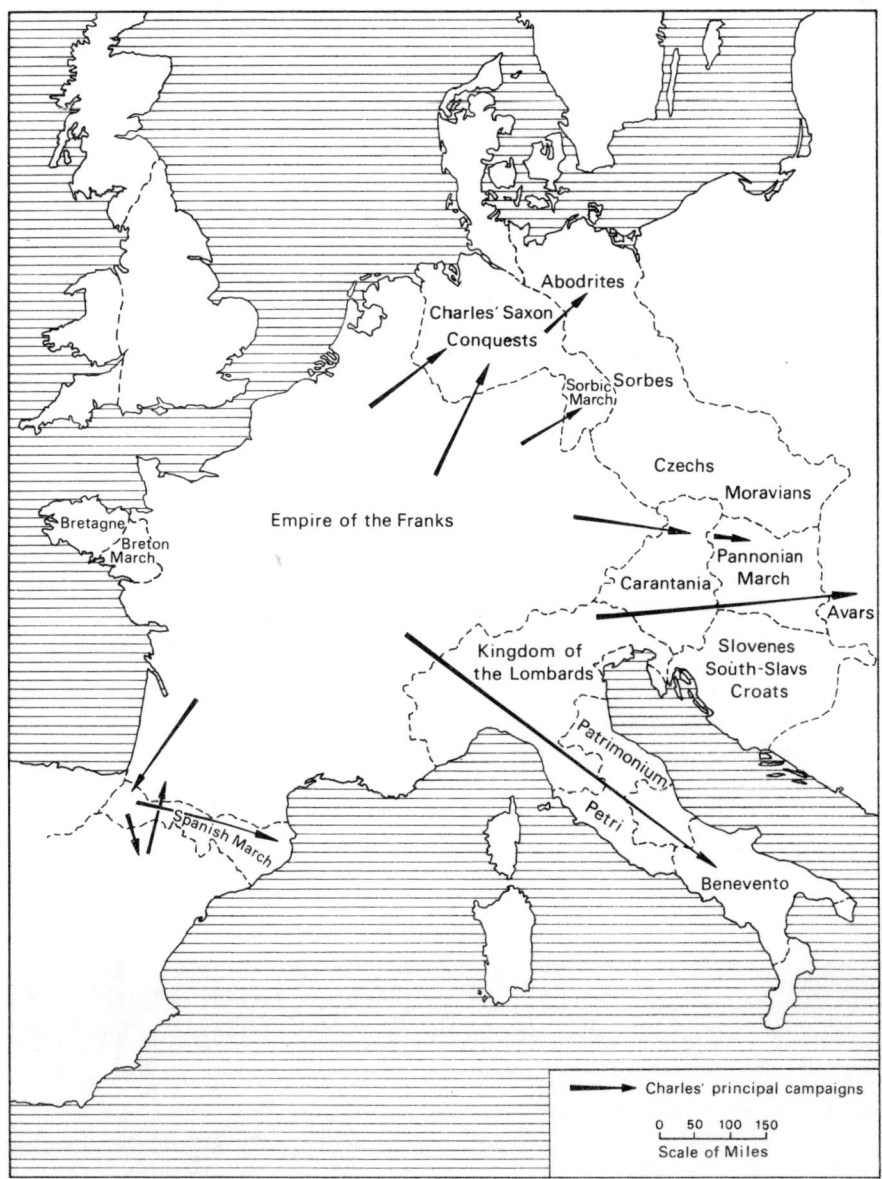

Fig. 1   The Empire of Charlemagne

Einhard, was interested not only in those aspects of learning which might be of immediate use in governmental administration, but also in poetry, the copying of biblical and Latin literary manuscripts, as well as the preservation of the heroic songs of the German tribes. He personally received instruction in Greek and Latin, and attempted—with little success—to teach himself to write. In 781 he met Alcuin and, by inviting him to his court, set in motion a series of events of the utmost importance for further cultural developments.

Fig. 2

While learning and the arts had almost vanished from continental Europe, they flourished in the British Isles. To a very considerable extent the continent received renewed intellectual stimulus from the schools and monasteries of England and Ireland. A case in point is Alcuin. Born in Northumberland around 735 and reared at the cathedral school of York under Archbishop Egbert, who had been a disciple of Bede at Jarrow, Alcuin was able to benefit from a powerful intellectual tradition. This heritage, aside from the usual emphasis on ecclesiastical history and Church doctrine, placed stress on the seven liberal arts, consisting of the *trivium* (grammar, rhetoric, dialectics) and the *quadrivium* (arithmetic, geometry, astronomy, music). When Archbishop Eanbald was installed at York in 780, Alcuin was head of the school as well as of the library of York Cathedral. During the same year, however, he was sent to Rome, to fetch the pallium for the new archbishop. On the return journey Alcuin met Charles at Parma. Not the least reason for Alcuin's acceptance of Charles' invitation was the scope to be given to the exercise of his talents—a scope rather limited at York, where, moreover, the political climate was not conducive to intellectual or pedagogical pursuits. After Alcuin's return to York, Archbishop Eanbald as well as King Elfwald of Northumbria readily gave him permission to depart, the latter hoping to gain prestige by the establishment of favourable connections with the powerful Frankish king.

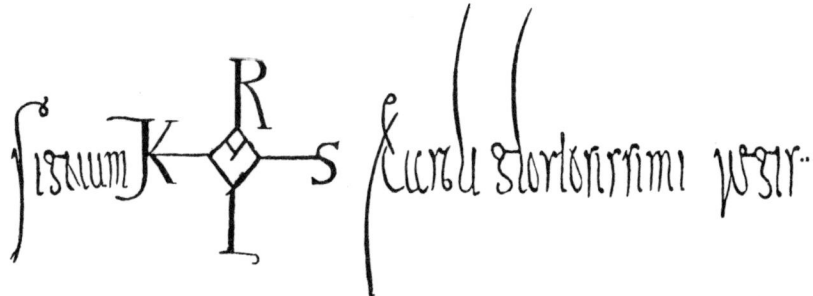

Fig. 2 Signature of Charlemagne on a deed from Kufstein dated August 31, 790. The actual signature consists of the lozenge containing the y-shaped angle. The surrounding words 'Signum + Caroli gloriosissimi regis' and the monogram were written by a scribe (after Jäger)

$$\begin{array}{c} R \\ K + S \\ L \end{array}$$

Alcuin's talents—pedagogical rather than creative—were precisely what was needed at the Frankish court. If the effort at centralization and the attempt to increase the efficiency of governmental administration were to be successful, administrators had to be trained. It was the basic function of the palace school, which Alcuin established at Charles' court, to provide the necessary education. The fact that this education rested on the fundament of the seven liberal arts accounts for their remaining the basis of medieval pedagogy. In an efficient administration, modelled after that of the Church, only Latin could serve as a means of communication, since no national common denominator was provided by any one vernacular. Moreover, since the affairs of the empire inevitably meshed with those of the Church, it was only natural that Latin should become the language of governmental officialdom. However, the influence of Alcuin's pedagogical endeavours was not limited to the training of Carolingian administrators in the language of politics, but led also to the establishment of Latin as the language of business and of learning, which it remained throughout the Middle Ages. Just as important as a standardization of the language of political and judicial

Fig. 3 The Christianization of Central Europe. The establishment of the principal monasteries and bishoprics, eighth to tenth century

administration was its graphic representation in written documents; hence the development of the clear, relatively standardized Carolingian uncial script at Charles' court.

But the palace school and the court of Charles were by no means the only centres of this so-called Carolingian renaissance. They were merely the starting points, just as Alcuin and Charles were not solely responsible for the revival of learning, but merely

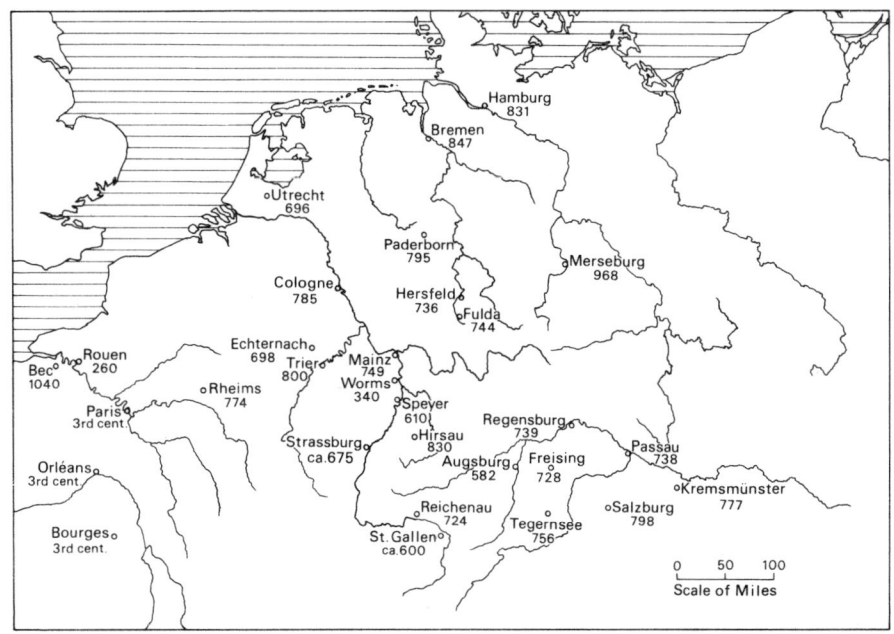

Fig. 4   Principal cultural centres, episcopal sees, monasteries, cathedral schools, during the eighth to tenth centuries

gave it the initial impetus. Alcuin, both as Charles' advisor and later as abbot of St Martin at Tours, was instrumental in the establishment and conduct of schools which, as a consequence of Charles' policies and direct legislation, sprang up throughout the empire. At these schools, connected either with Benedictine monasteries—St Martin at Tours, Fulda, Reichenau—or with cathedrals—Paris, Rheims, Chartres—intellectual and artistic activity continued after Alcuin's and Charles' death. It was carried on largely by scholars and artists whose cultural descent can be traced, however indirectly, to Alcuin and his fellow scholars at Charles' court, such as Paul the Deacon, author of a History of the Lombards, the Latinist Peter of Pisa, Theodulf, poet and bishop of Orleans, Angilbert, another poet and archbishop of Lyons, and Charles' biographer Einhard.

Figs. 3, 4

One of Alcuin's own students was primarily responsible for carrying on the tradition in Germany: Hrabanus Maurus (c. 776–856), abbot of Fulda, later archbishop of Mainz, was, in fact, more gifted than his teacher. As is to be expected from a pupil of Alcuin, he stressed the study of the liberal arts and of pagan authors—not, of course, for their own sake, but as conducive to a better understanding of the Christian faith. With his *De universo*, Hrabanus followed in the footsteps of Isidore of Seville and of Bede, whose encyclopedic method also provided the basis for Alcuin's pedagogical programme. The work of Hrabanus Maurus, both in its organizational and pedagogical aspects, was carried on in Germany by Hrabanus' pupils, Walafrid Strabo (c. 810–849), abbot of Reichenau, to whom a standard gloss on the Scriptures was ascribed until recently, and Otfrid (c. 800–870), monk of Weissenburg and author of a story of Christ's life in Old High German.[2]

The greatest intellect of the Carolingian era, surpassing both the initiators as well as the transmitters of the 'Carolingian renaissance', was John the Scot. John, or Duns Scotus Erigena, was born c. 810 in Ireland, i.e. *Scotia maior*, and taught at the court of Charles the Bald. In contrast to the primarily pedagogical and organizational gift which distinguished Alcuin and most other Carolingian scholars of note, John's talent was creative. His thought, nourished by the tradition of the Church Fathers and Latin culture as well as by the mysticism of the Greek neoplatonists Denys the Areopagite and Maximus the Confessor, was of the utmost consequence for the development of medieval philosophy. His principal work, *De divisione naturae*, reflects neoplatonist influences in his view of nature as a 'theophany', God's revelation of Himself through creation. Everything that exists, therefore, is a participation in God's nature as creation expresses it. This concept, which was to play an important role in later forms of mystical thought, embodied also—as basis for a hierarchy of existence dependent on the relative proximity of the various forms of existence to God—the essence of that most characteristic of medieval modes of thought: gradualism.[3]

Structurally related to gradualism is the idea of beauty set forth in the tract *De divinis nominibus* by Denys the Areopagite, which influenced its translator, John the Scot, and determined the medieval perception of art in general.[4] Perfection and beauty are identical; thus demons are to some extent beautiful, since they are not totally imperfect. Nothing which exists is totally imperfect; total imperfection is non-existence. All perception, therefore, is a partaking of some degree of beauty, reflecting 'partial' perfection; this stimulates the desire for absolute perfection, absolute beauty, and these belong to a realm beyond the reach of sin. John the Scot elaborated on the analogous relationship between the perceivable beauty of objects and the supra-natural realm of perfection: 'the entire universe becomes a powerful light which is composed of many parts, as of many lamps, in order to reveal the pure images of intelligible things and perceive them with the eyes of reason' (*Super ierarchiam coelestam S. Dion.* I, 1). Here the symbolism and allegorism which dominate medieval aesthetics until the fifteenth century find their initial systematic justification.

The Carolingian state represented a fusion of the ancient Roman ideal of a centrally administered universal empire with agricultural, post-migratory, tribal socio-economic reality. While this state disintegrated, the forms of subservience to the central power were preserved, providing a basis for the subsequent development of feudalism. In fact, the origin of feudalism is Carolingian, if it is regarded as essentially a system of relationships in which the lord provides his vassals with the means of rendering military service on condition that they bind themselves to serve when called upon.[5] The introduction of the stirrup in the eighth century brought about a revolution in warfare, which presupposes a rudimentary form of feudalism. The military significance of the stirrup as lateral support for the rider, enabling him to act in unison with his mount, was quickly recog-

Fig. 5   David riding out against his enemies. From the Psalterium Aureum, *St Gallen, ninth century (after Middleton)*

nized. The spear held, guided, and thrust by the hand of an insecurely mounted horseman was now replaced with the lance, cradled and guided by the right arm of the cavalryman securely mounted on his horse, and deriving its power of impact not from the rider's hand, but from the motion of his charging mount. The eighth century witnessed a sharp increase in the use of cavalry by the Frankish armies. The equipment of a mounted warrior, however, was expensive: he needed a horse, weapons, feed for his horse, and remounts. It has been estimated that the military equipment for one horseman cost about twenty oxen. The extensive re-allotments of confiscated Church lands by Charlemagne's grandfather, Charles Martel (d. 741), and his father, Pipin (d. 768), as well as his own attempt to raise mounted warriors from the poorer freemen by commanding them to form groups, each group to equip one of its members, testify to the formation of essentially feudal relationships to support great numbers of horsemen.

The Carolingian state, a fusion of the Roman imperial idea with contemporary circumstances, has its parallel in the intellectual currents of the period. These represented a confluence of the classical, primarily Latin tradition with the contemporary intellectual climate of Christianity, whose demands it served and whose content it continued to mould throughout the Middle Ages.

The same can be said of the Carolingian arts. The art of the Roman empire, in contrast to the classical art of Greece, was predominantly narrative, concerned with the telling of a story, be it in painting or sculpture. The order prevailing in a coherent narrative is necessarily temporal: that which is told is imagined as happening in a time sequence. This stress upon the temporal of necessity excludes purely spatial representation, which, being based on vanishing-point perspective, must emanate from a fixed viewpoint. Hence also the artificiality of a frame around a narrative depiction: its function of defining a space to be represented has no place in an art not concerned with space. Since the representation of spacial relationships does not serve as organizing principle in narrative art, order and design devolve upon the organization of the picture surface, conceived as two-dimensional. Carolingian artists took over a limited number of types of representation and organization of the surface from antiquity, which they used within the context of Christian symbolism for narrative, didactic purposes, conceiving of all art as serving the purpose of 'memoria rerum gestarum.'[6]

Fig. 5

Medieval Civilization in Germany

Plate 3

Plates 5, 6

Plate 4

A good example of the complete negation of space is afforded by the miniature of the Elders of the Apocalypse adoring the Lamb in the Munich Codex Aureus from St Emmeram (*c.* 870). This breaks entirely with the conventions of spatial representation of antiquity while making use of late antique and Byzantine patterns of portrayal. The effect is produced by the surface pattern of the hemicircle of the Elders, each executing the same gesture, around the Lamb, which, itself enclosed in a circle, floats in an abstract sky. Equally obvious is the negation of space as an organizing principle in the effigy, a pictorial genre which was to be of the greatest significance for medieval art in general. The miniature of the emperor Lothar in his Gospel may serve as an example. The importance of the figure within its context is indicated by its size and centrality. This emphasis on the two-dimensional at the expense of treatment in depth meant that the distinction between images seen in perspective and purely surface ornament tended to disappear. The elimination of this difference was aided by the continued influence of pre-Carolingian Germanic stylized ornamental art, with its stress on braided or interlaced patterns, zigzags, etc. The sacramentary written for Bishop Drogo of Metz between 826 and 855 documents this transition in the treatment of initials. The medieval tradition of using an initial as frame for a figure illustration is here first represented. The letter is converted from a geometric figure to a representation of an object such as a frame, a trellis, or similar three-dimensionally conceived structural element. Within this metaphorically used letter, within this framework, or supported by it, are figures, human or animal, or simply flora, whose relationship to the trellis or frame is ambiguous: the three-dimensionality of the figures suggests that they are to be conceived of as a scene observed through the frame. However, their relationship to the frame—or rather the lack of such a relationship, owing to the conflict between the symbolic and representational functions of the letter, and the clash between this ambiguity and the figures within the frame—makes it equally likely that the frame merely serves to delimit the picture surface. It would thus fulfil a purely linear function and convert the space-depth illusion into the surface-time conception which characterizes medieval art. In short, here and in Carolingian art in general one already encounters the basic characteristic of medieval art as a whole: it is not to be 'looked at' as an illusion; it is to be 'read', much as the written word which occupies the surface of a page and functions as a symbol.[7]

Carolingian architecture, predominantly religious, reflected to a considerable degree the clerical reforms, particularly those of the cathedral clergy, who, as at Metz and elsewhere, were made subject to monastic discipline. This affected the topography of cathedrals, since the clergy had to be provided with chapter houses, refectories, and oratories. On the premises occupied by these churches and their adjuncts there later arose monumental Romanesque and Gothic cathedrals which entirely changed the face of the towns. The Carolingian churches themselves were built for the most part on the basilican plan. A most important exception is the imperial chapel at Aachen, which was designed on an octagonal plan with galleries. In this architectural masterpiece, the builder Odo of Metz achieved perfect stability of the dome with a minimal number of supports and anticipated the solution of the roofing problem by three hundred years. Here, as in other Carolingian churches, ornamentation of surfaces rather than sculpture played a dominant decorative role. At Aachen a mosaic twelve feet high, depicting Christ with the twenty-four Elders of the Apocalypse at His feet, covered the interior of the dome.

Plate 9

Among architectural innovations of significance for later developments are the construction of crypts, as at St Germain at Auxerre, under the raised east end of the sanctuary, the development of the 'Benedictine apse' from the three parallel apses, and the ambulatory.

The literary production of the Carolingian period reflects a fusion—similar to that in art—of Germanic formal tradition and Christian content in the case of vernacular literature, and of late Latin tradition and Christian purpose in the predominantly learned Latin literature. Perhaps the only examples of purely pagan literature are the two alliterative Merseburg charms, dating from *c.* 800. Both charms call upon the aid of members of the pagan Germanic pantheon, the one to aid in healing a horse's foot, the other in freeing captives.

Of considerably greater significance, however, is the *Hildebrandslied*. An alliterative lay of the eighth or very early ninth century, transmitted on two parchment leaves, it is the one remnant in German literature of purely heroic poetry, and as such may be an example of the type of poem contained in Charlemagne's collection of Germanic heroic song—if such a collection ever existed. The language in which it is transmitted presents a problem: it is a mixture of High and Low German, which makes speculation about the reasons for this linguistic confusion as inviting as it is inconclusive. The theory which most closely fits the textual facts is that this linguistic mixture is the result of an unsuccessful attempt to render a High German poem in Low German. The palaeographical aspects of the manuscript also raise problems: it was written by two scribes, and while it is for the most part a moderately good example of Carolingian minuscule, it also contains some insular forms. It is pointless to attempt a dating or an exact characterization of the 'original form' of the *Hildebrandslied*, since its formulaic content clearly marks it as orally composed and orally transmitted virtually up to the time when it took shape in our manuscript. However, it can be said with considerable certainty that it is native to High German rather than Low German territory.

The story has as its theme the battle to the death between father and son, which is to be found, in one form or another, in the Greek tale of Odysseus and Telegonos, the Persian Sohrab and

Rustum, the Irish Conlach and Cuchulain, and many others. The old warrior Hildebrand, returning with his men from the wars of his lord Theodoric against Odoacer, is confronted by his son Hadubrand at the head of his followers. Hildebrand asks Hadubrand's identity by enquiring after the name of his father. Hadubrand believes him to be long dead, and suspects Hildebrand of trickery when the latter, realizing that he is speaking to his son, attempts to win his confidence by offering him armbands as tokens of his peaceful intentions. By his forceful rejection of Hildebrand's approaches, Hadubrand makes a battle to the death between himself and his father unavoidable. Hildebrand, realizing that either he must die by the hand of his son or himself kill him, cries out to God to witness the enormity of the situation. After a very brief, defiant exchange, father and son begin to fight—thus far our manuscript. But neither the evidence of the later Icelandic *Ásmundarsaga*, nor an extrapolation from our knowledge of pagan Germanic culture with its respect for experience and age is necessary in order to arrive at the only possible conclusion of the poem. Not only is Hildebrand referred to specifically as the older, more experienced of the two, but he also takes the initiative throughout the poem and is perfectly aware of the situation and its demands. Moreover—and this is perhaps the most obvious indication—within this context, which permits none but a tragic ending, only Hildebrand knows whom he is fighting. Were his son to be victorious, the victory would be empty, even absurd, for he is under the impression that his opponent is not his father, but a treacherous old Hun. Although the *Hildebrandslied* obviously is a remnant of preChristian heroic poetry, it already shows signs of adaptation to the new cultural environment. Specifically pagan elements are lacking, and Hildebrand's outcry to God is directed at the Christian omnipotent, omnipresent God.

For another instance—and another form—of adaptation of preChristian Germanic poetry to the new cultural determinants one

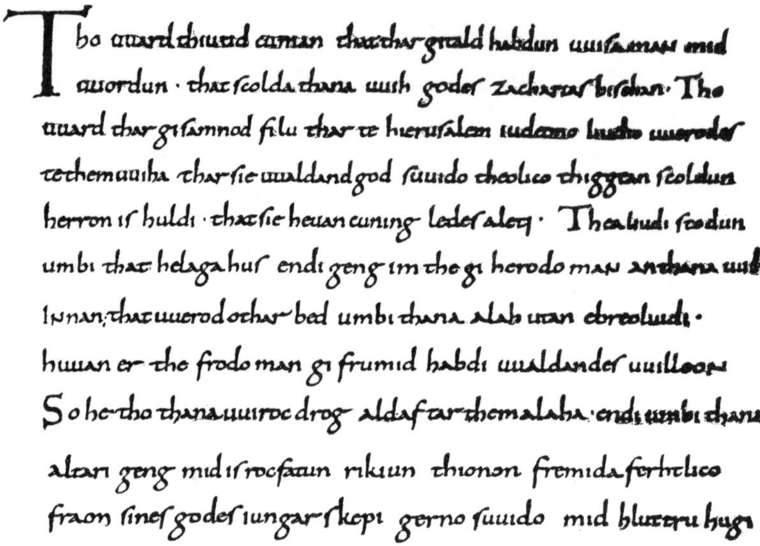

Fig. 6 A page from the Munich manuscript of the Heliant, *ninth century (after Nadler)*

Fig. 6

must turn to Old Saxon poetry. The Saxons were the most refractory of the tribes which Charles sought to convert to Christianity, and it is to them that the so-called *Heliant* addresses itself. The basis for this life of Christ is the *Diatessaron* of Tatian, a Syrian of the second century. The *Heliant* was written during the reign of Charles' son Louis the Pious (814–840), for the expressed purpose of making the teachings of the Christian religion available to the broad masses not versed in Latin. The matter of the Gospels, however, was adapted to the exigencies of both the Germanic oral tradition in poetry, and the still half-pagan cultural environment for which the work was destined. The poem exhibits all the stylistic characteristics associated with oral composition, i.e. with the productions of the scops: the use of formulae, adaptation of traditional themes, and so forth. Just as Caedmon adapted the traditional heroic style to the new Christian matter in Anglo-Saxon literature almost two hundred

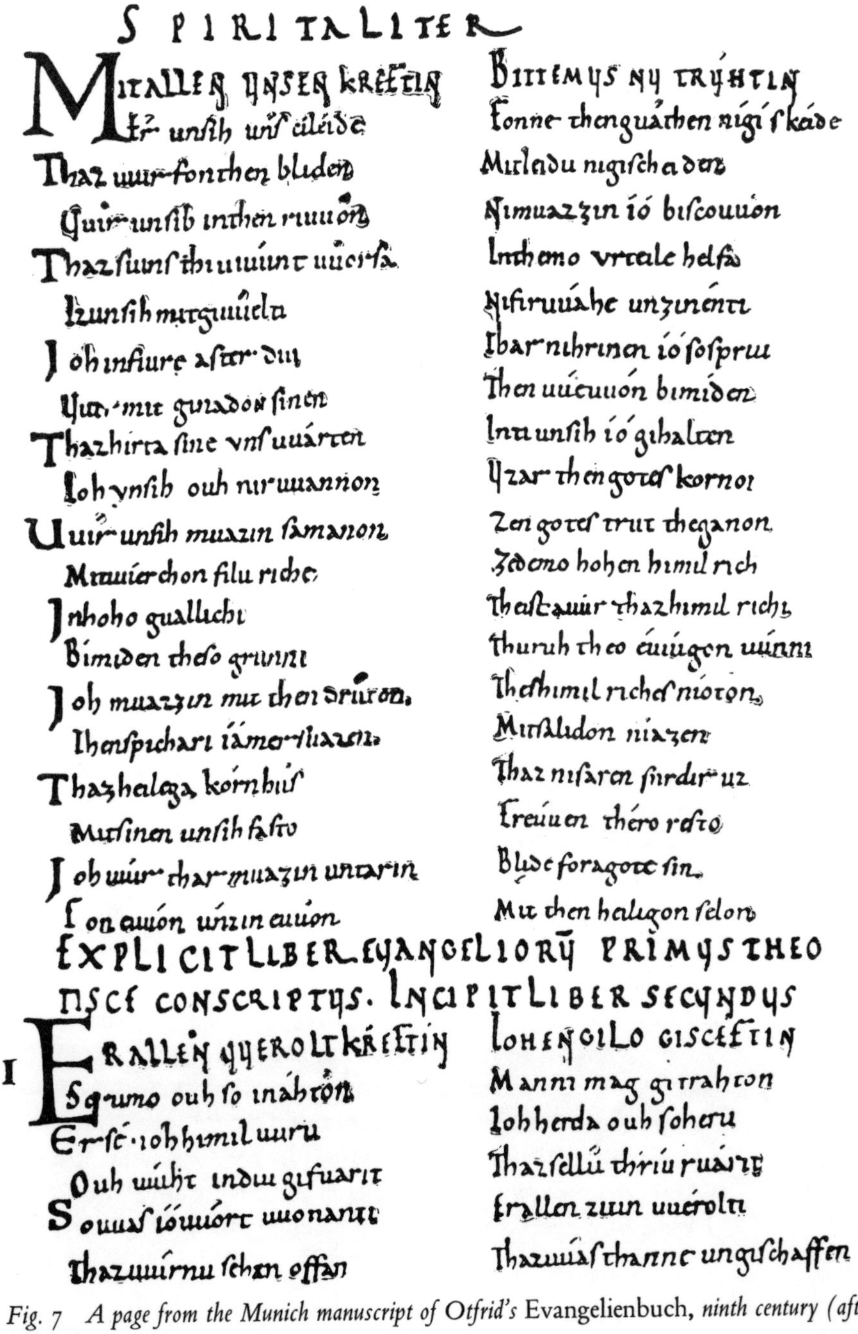

SPIRITALITER

Mit allen unseren kreftin | Bittemes nu truhtin
er unsih uuolelade | sonne thenguathen nigisskade
Thaz uuir fon then blidon | Muotadu nigischadoz
Guir unsih in then riuuon | Nimuazzin io biscouuon
Thaz sumis thiu uuint uuerfa | In themo urteile helfa
Izunsih mitguuielu | Nifiruuahe unzenenti
Joh in sture aftar diu | Ibar nihrinen io sosprui
Uuar mit guradon sinen | Then uuicuuon bimidez
Thaz hirta sine uns uuarten | Intu unsih io gihalten
Joh unsih ouh nir uuannon | Yzar then gotes kornoz
Uuir unsih muazin samanon | Zen gotes truit theganon
Mauuerchon filu riche | Zedemo hohen himil rich
In hoho guallichi | Theist uuir thaz himil richi
Bimiden thes gruinzi | Thuruh theo euuigen uuinni
Joh muazin mit then druton | Thes himil riches nuozon
Thenspichari iamor thazen | Mit salidon niazen
Thaz haloga kornhus | Thaz nisaren surdir uz
Musinen unsih fasto | Freuuen thero rasto
Joh uuir thar muazin untarin | Blide foragote sin
Son auon uuizin auion | Mit then heligon selon

EXPLICIT LIBER EUANGELIORU PRIMUS THEO
TISCE CONSCRIPTUS. INCIPIT LIBER SECUNDUS

I Er allen queroltkreftin | Lohen ollo giscaftin
   Esgrumo ouh so inahton | Manni mag girrahton
   Erst iohhimil uuru | Iohherda ouh soheru
   Ouh uuiht indiu gifuarit | Thaz sellu thriu ruarit
   Souuas touuort uuonanti | Frallen zuuin uueroltı
   Thazuuirnu schon offan | Thazuuasthanne ungischaffen

Fig. 7 *A page from the Munich manuscript of Otfrid's* Evangelienbuch, *ninth century (after Nadler)*

years before, the poet of the *Heliant* used the formulae and themes of pre-Christian, orally composed heroic poetry to render the matter of the Gospels. The result is a presentation of the story of the Gospels in terms familiar and understandable to a public not yet fully converted: Christ is a mighty warrior chieftain, of noble birth; the apostles are his men, likewise of noble lineage. The Sermon on the Mount is introduced as if it were a Germanic 'thing', i.e. a council. This does not mean, however, that the poem actually was composed orally. The sophisticated structure of the whole makes this currently still common assumption untenable. It was composed, as is to be expected, by a literate poet, who availed himself of the method of the non-literate poet of heroic song simply because the style of the latter was familiar to the audience for whom the message was destined: the non-literate public. The content, the message, was adapted to the scope of understanding of this audience, and the form, the presentation of the message, conformed to the style to which that audience was accustomed.

Fig. 7

A different sort of narrative of Christ's life is the *Liber Evangeliorum* of Otfrid, monk of Weissenburg (*c.* 800–870). This first transmitted instance of end-rhyming poetry in Old High German reflects the Latin Christian tradition as represented by St Augustine, Bede, and Alcuin—Otfrid was a student of Hrabanus Maurus—in the allegorical commentary interwoven in the story of the Gospels, as well as in the narrative itself, for which the Vulgate was the basis. This tradition received Old High German garb to serve the interests of the Frankish Church: to oppose heroic poetry with a Christian epic in the Frankish tongue.

The converse relationship of content, form, and language exists in the case of the Latin epic poem *Waltharius manu fortis*, which now appears to have originated in the mid-ninth century. The narrative matter is native to the heroic Germanic epic: it consists of the exploits of Walther of Aquitaine and Hildegund of Burgundy, who, on their flight from Hunnish captivity, are confronted by Gunther and Hagen, who intend to rob them. In style, however, this poem in hexameters is modelled on Vergil's *Aeneid*.

In the various genres of Christian writing—whether the purpose be erudition, such as in glosses and glossaries, or more generally didactic, as for instance in the *Ludwigslied*, celebrating the victory of Louis III over the Normans at Saucourt (881), or in the fragmentary *Muspilli*, describing the fate of the soul after death and doomsday—the main currents of Carolingian culture manifest themselves in the manner observable in the other arts and in intellectual development in general: the amalgamation of certain aspects of classical traditions of form with Christian content—an amalgamation in which both form and content are changed into something new.

Fig. 8 Coin of the reign of Charlemagne, minted in Trier. Legend: 'Karolus Imp(erator) Aug(ustus)' (after Jäger). 2:1

Economic developments and the social fabric seem at first glance to exhibit characteristics which differ from this developmental pattern. Commerce and the cities, which still played a relatively vital role during the Merovingian period, were almost non-existent as socio-economic factors. Trade consisted primarily of barter, and the domains of the nobles became less dependent

Fig. 9 Signature of Louis the German on a deed from Frankfurt a. M. dated 87–(?). Legend: '*Signum*+ *domni kludovvici serenissimi regis*' *(after Jäger)*

on each other as well as on the imperial power, both economically and politically. At the same time, agricultural production increased with the replacement of two-field by three-field cultivation, which made possible the continuous cultivation of two-thirds, rather than one half, of arable land, while one third lay fallow. Among the most important results of this innovation were far-reaching improvements in human as well as animal nutrition. The introduction of the modern horse-collar, enabling peasants to·cultivate their land more efficiently by using horses rather than oxen for ploughing, contributed further to the economic health of this fragmented agricultural society. The resulting surplus of agricultural products not only reduced the danger of famine, but made possible an increased division of labour on the domains of the nobles. Peasants no longer needed to produce their own agricultural tools; they were manufactured with increasing frequency by tradesmen who were not involved in agricultural production.[8] These developments, adding to the economic independence of individual domains, gave impetus to the growth of political particularism. The imperial power, however, was viewed as a re-establishment of universal order through a revival of the *Imperium Romanum*, coupled with Christianity and the duty to defend, uphold, and increase it as well as the power of the Church. The decentralization of secular power which took place at the same time and despite all the efforts of Charlemagne, and which gathered speed as those efforts decreased under the later Carolingians, led directly to the development of an intricately structured feudal order with all its socio-political implications.

One can generalize in characterizing the Carolingian era as having accomplished a fusion of classical traditions on the one hand, and remnants of pre-Christian Germanic tribal culture on the other, with the demands—intellectual and political—of Christianity. This fusion resulted in the creation of new forms of thought and action: the fundaments of medieval Western civilization. The forms which medieval culture took in Germany developed from these fundaments and evolved in their own characteristic manner, but always on the basis of the cultural denominators common to European medieval civilization as a whole.

CHAPTER II

The Saxon and Salian Dynasties and the Age of Romanesque

CENTRALIZATION and political stabilization were the principal aims—attained to a considerable degree—of the reigns of the Ottos.[1] The power vacuums created by the disintegration of the Carolingian empire were filled principally by the ducal dynasties, among whose members Arnulf of Bavaria and Burkhard of Swabia were pre-eminent. The reign of the Franconian king Conrad (911–918), who succeeded the last of the East Frankish Carolingians, Louis the Child, did little to strengthen the monarchy, although his election by the territorial magnates proceeded smoothly enough. The combination of his stubborn insistence on royal powers and a marked lack of success in battle—in the West to recover control of Lorraine, in the East to repel the Magyars—caused the nobility to stiffen their resistance to the Crown. The aristocracy consolidated its power and pursued an increasingly anti-monarchical policy, strengthening the position it had won in the absence of a strong Carolingian royal policy. When, therefore, the Saxon Henry I received the royal insignia at the behest of the dying Conrad in 919, the fundamental problem facing him and his son Otto after him, was the assertion of royal authority over the expanding power of the dukes. The fact that Henry was designated king by his predecessor, rather than elected by the dukes, already contributed to the establishment of royal supremacy. Moreover, the Saxon king adhered to the Frankish monarchic tradition and ceased to identify solely with his own Saxon inheritance. Rising above dynastic provincialism, he made an identification of his monarchy with its Carolingian predecessor easy.

Fig. 10   Signature of Otto I on a deed given before the walls of Ravenna in 970. Legend: 'Signum domni ottonis magni et invictissimi imperatoris augusti' (after Jäger)

Swabia at this point represented the greatest danger to royal power, since it, along with Bavaria, was in a position to conduct its own foreign policy because of its involvement in Burgundian and Italian affairs. By the second year of his reign, however, Henry was in full control of the crown properties in Swabia, the Church gradually came under direct royal influence, and the king appointed a new duke, a Frank, thus binding the ducal office to the crown. At the coronation of Otto I (936), the re-established supremacy of the monarch over the dukes was symbolized by the latters' acting as royal servants in carrying out their ceremonial duties during the festivities. The significance of Otto's choice of the chapel of Charlemagne at Aachen for the ceremony also cannot have been lost on the nobility.

Throughout the reign of the Saxon dynasty, the Crown firmly allied itself with the Church. It is this alliance which is the single most potent factor contributing to the victory of the monarchy over the territorial magnates. The Church was the natural and logical ally of the Crown: in supplanting the local nobility in matters of local government, it did not pose the problems and dangers inherent in a system of hereditary succession. In addition, the clergy was still the only educated class, and therefore uniquely equipped to discharge administrative duties.

The exercise of administrative functions by the Church was a unifying factor and helped to secure the territories won during the eastward expansion which began in the reign of Henry I and continued for some three centuries. Otto's achievement of decisively defeating the Magyars at the battle of Lechfeld in 955 eliminated a grave threat, but enabled him merely to secure reconquered territory. The acquisition of new land occurred in the north. Using Henry's conquests of Brandenburg on the Havel, the march of Schleswig, and particularly the Bugberg at Meissen, as points of departure, Otto I systematically extended German domination by establishing military strongpoints—as Henry had done before him—in the Thuringian march under Margrave Gero, and in Lower Saxony under Hermann Billung. One cannot, however, speak of any significant degree of colonization in either case. German expansion into these areas had simply the aim of subjugating the Slav inhabitants and, wherever possible, exacting tribute from neighbouring tribes.

The opposition of the Slavic tribes to the German conquerors was considerable, and the history of the conquest of Slav territory is one long tale of ruthlessness and treachery. The lives of the margraves Gero and Hermann Billung yield a variety of deeds characterizing the German eastward thrust. One example will suffice: having failed to break the opposition of the Slavs of the Elbe, to whose subjugation he devoted twenty-seven years, Gero invited thirty of their princes to a feast and had them murdered. This caused a general revolt, and a Saxon army was defeated. Even Saxon armies under the personal leadership of Otto I had little success against the Slavs of the Elbe, and only achieved domination over Brandenburg and Havelberg, which were no

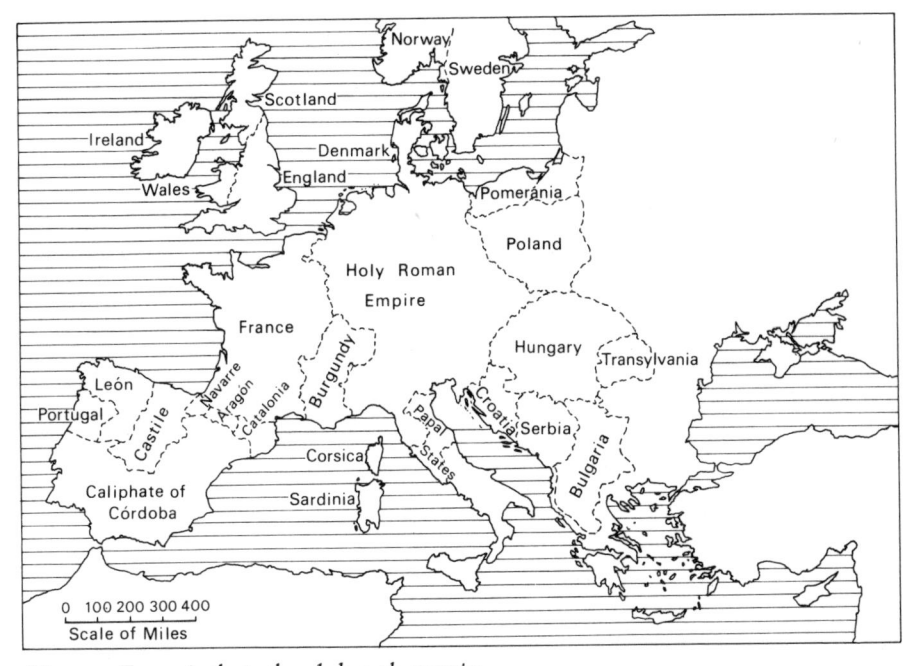

Fig. 11   Europe in the tenth and eleventh centuries

longer in German hands, as a result of the treachery of the Slav prince Tugumir. Bribed while a prisoner of the Saxons, Tugumir, after murdering his nephew, a prince of the Havel-Slavs, had turned the fortress of Brandenburg over to the Saxons.

The German expansion into Slav territory was accompanied by the establishment of new ecclesiastical sees, which constituted the necessary administrative network. The foundation of these sees reveals the ambitious plans of Otto I for the Christianization of the Slavs. A particularly clear example is the establishment of the archbishopric of Magdeburg without an eastern boundary.

The Slav population revolted in 982 and ended German domination except in Magdeburg and on the Danish border. Whereas eastward expansion stopped for the time being, the monarchy profited from the colonization of Thuringia and Franconia, and its prestige increased: in 962 Otto I was invested with the title

47

Fig. 11

Imperator et Augustus. From this point on, German policy and imperial policy, the interests of the empire and the papacy, of Germany and Italy, become inextricably involved with one another.

It has been aptly remarked that in the process of establishing and securing his imperial power Otto I neither found himself in, nor sought, the position of his imperial predecessor Charlemagne; if his position is to be compared to that of a Carolingian, then that of Lothar I provides the closest parallel. The disintegration of the Carolingian Middle Kingdom—Italy, Burgundy, Provence, Lorraine—after the death of Charles the Fat (888) not only created a highly volatile situation on the borders of Otto's kingdom, but involved the two most restless components of that kingdom—Bavaria and Swabia—in Italian power politics. This involvement was of the greatest danger to the German monarchy, a danger which Henry I had already recognized when he intervened in the affairs of Lorraine and Burgundy. The security of German territory depended on German control of the areas to the south and south-west. It was the essentially nationalistic aim of providing such security, rather than imperialistic ambition, which led Otto I to Rome to seek the imperial crown.

Fig. 12 Coin of the reign of Otto I, minted in Strassburg. Legend: 'Otto Rex Pacif(icua)—Argenta Uoto' (Bishop Udo of Strassburg) (after Jäger)

The Saxon and Salian Dynasties

A reaction against Otto's hegemony over Italy made its appearance during his lifetime and gathered strength under his successors. He had left much governmental power in the hands of the Italian bishops, who could better be relied upon than the counts. The allegiance of the bishops, however, was only temporary. They gradually extended their powers over the monasteries under royal protection, which, with their assets in land and labour, had been extremely important to the monarchy. The deterioration of the royal power in Italy became obvious after the defeat of Otto II near Cotrone in Calabria (982), when a series of rebellions against his administrators took place. After the death of Otto II in 983, and the accession of Otto III (983–1002) to the throne, imperial policy in Italy was completely revised. German administrators *(ministeriales)* were employed on Church lands in an effort to halt their gradual expropriation by the petty nobility, and while renewed emphasis was placed on the protection of the properties of Church and Crown, the Italian episcopate was replaced by German administrators in the role of guardians over these properties.

Plate 13

After the death of Otto III, however, the Italian policy of the emperors reverted to the pre-Ottonian stage. The imperial power in Italy waned as the inconsistency of its policies increased. Henry II (1002–1024) relied heavily on the episcopate, Conrad II (1024–1039) on the provincial feudal lords, whereas Henry III (1039–1056) again supported the bishops.

Imperial policies regarding Italy and the empire at large varied, but one common denominator characterizes the rule of the Saxon dynasty as a whole: whatever those policies were at any given time, they were pursued not for the sake of some nebulous notion of a universal empire, but always for the sake of German interests. Not the least benefit to those interests, and indeed to central European interests in general, derived from the imperial title of the German kings, which set them apart from other monarchs. Since the reign of Conrad II the imperial title

Fig. 13 Imperial seal of Conrad II from a deed given at Goslar, February 19, 1031. The similarity of the face with the profile on a contemporary coin suggests that this may be a rare instance of portraiture (after Jäger)

became, in principle, hereditary: the title *'Rex Romanorum in Imperatorem promovendus'* was borne by the German kings before their investiture with the imperial regalia by the Pope. Thus the German realm and the *'Imperium Romanum'* merged under the aegis of the German monarchy.

One of the most significant results of the victory of the principle of heredity over that of election was a reduction in political regionalism. Had the provincial magnates been able to maintain their power, an increase in regionalism would have been inevitable. But the social and economic stability ushered in by the successes of the Ottonian monarchy brought about a revival of commerce which contributed to the breakdown of regionalism.

It has been estimated that during the Carolingian era there were sixty to seventy market-towns which were the focal points of trade.[2] At the beginning of the eleventh century there were between two and three hundred such towns between the Rhine and the area of the Elbe and Saale. The most important exports were salt from Halle, Lüneburg, and Hall, silver, copper, and lead from the mines near Goslar, wines from the Rhine and Moselle valleys, Frisian cloth, and Slav slaves. Imports included,

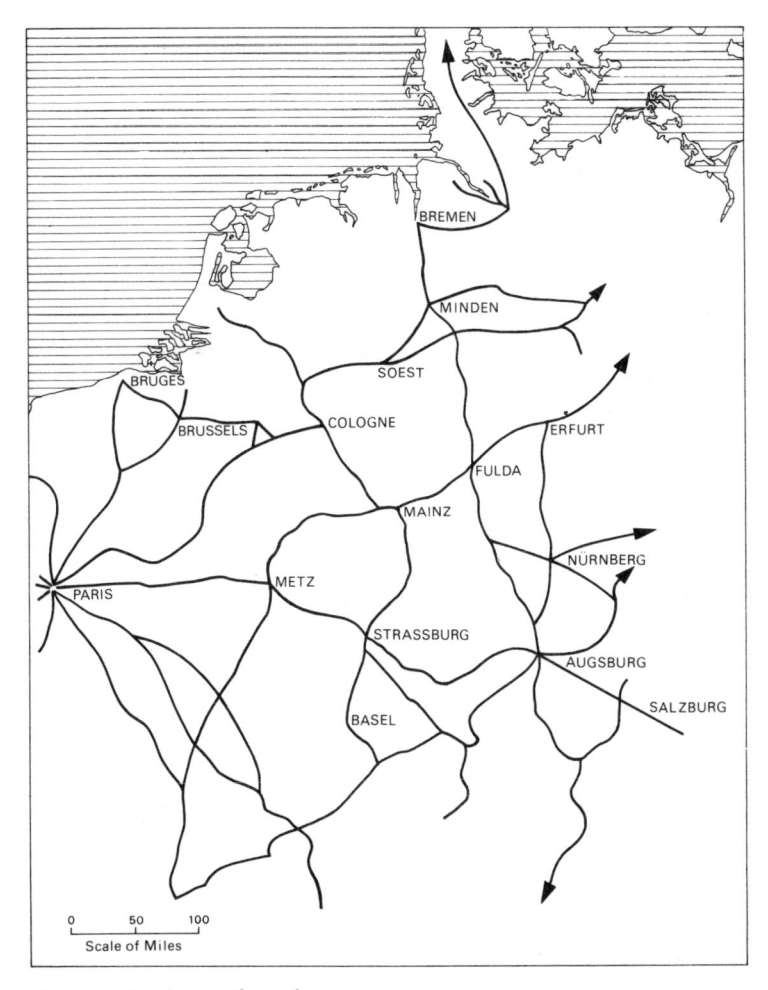

Fig. 14   Road network, tenth century

from the North, furs, amber, honey, wax, silver; from the Mediterranean area, spices, incense and jewelled weapons. The principal arteries of commerce included not only the few high-roads and great rivers, the Danube, Rhine, and Elbe, but also smaller waterways such as the Moselle, Neckar, Main, and Diemel, which acted as strands in a unifying network.

Fig. 14

The principal weakness of the Ottonian monarchy lay in the fact that its governmental structure rested upon shifting foundations. Both in the royal appointments of dukes and in the use of the Church as an administrative tool and political ally, the king had to rely on the personal loyalty of dukes and clerics. He therefore appointed relatives to high office in the Church as well as to the duchies: Bruno, brother of Otto I, for instance, became archbishop of Cologne, his son William, archbishop of Mainz. Bruno was also, for a time, Duke of Lorraine, while William, in 965, became imperial chancellor.

Such arrangements were necessarily temporary expedients and could not serve as substitutes for a coherent policy over a long period of time. The change from the reliance of Henry II on the bishops at court rather than on the aristocratic episcopacy and the Benedictine abbots, to Conrad II's favouring of the counts and Henry III's reversion to an imperial theocracy, was part of a series of attempts to establish a cohesive policy. Neither reliance on the ecclesiastical establishment nor dependence on the lesser nobility proved practicable. The former failed because the interests of the higher clergy conflicted with those of the Crown, the latter, because a tight feudal structure, in which all freemen were vassals, was still lacking in German society. Therefore the dissatisfaction of the lower nobility with their vassalage to the higher nobility did not necessarily align them with the interests of the Crown.

The survival, in Germany, of a relatively large number of free men, lords as well as peasants, wary of all attempts to impose vassalage upon them, required the king—or any lord in need of administrative officers and knights—to turn to the *ministeriales*. Although they were rewarded with land, this was not regarded as a fief, but as a servile tenure, and their persons were considered unfree. With the growth of commerce and the increasing complexity of governmental administration, however, the *ministeriales* came to form a class of the highest social, political, and

Figs. 15, 16 Above: signature of Henry II on a deed dated Kaufungen, 1016. Legend: 'Signum domni Henrici invic/tissimi'. Right: coin of the reign of Henry II, minted in Augsburg. Legend: 'Heinricus R.—Augusta Civ.' 2 : 1 (both after Jäger)

cultural significance, and many of them rose to prominence. Conrad II began to employ *ministeriales* on a systematic basis, and under Henry IV (1056–1106) their employment as administrators had already become established policy.

With the aid of these trusted servants of the Crown the generally successful efforts to recoup crown lands expropriated by the nobility were begun by Conrad II and continued by Henry III and Henry IV. Henry IV consolidated these gains by having a survey made of the crown lands, by enclosing forests and wastelands, and by making use of the Rammelsberg silver mines near Goslar as a source of bullion, thus increasing the economic resources of the monarchy and obviating an extensive reduction of royal domains through grants of land. Moreover, Saxony and Thuringia were dotted with castles garrisoned by royal *ministeriales* to protect the interests of the Crown. The centre of this network of fortresses was Goslar, where there had been a royal castle since the reign of Otto III. It was not far from the silver mines, and under Henry IV, who intended to use it as a permanent capital, it became 'clarissimum illud regni domicilium'.

Plates 15, 16

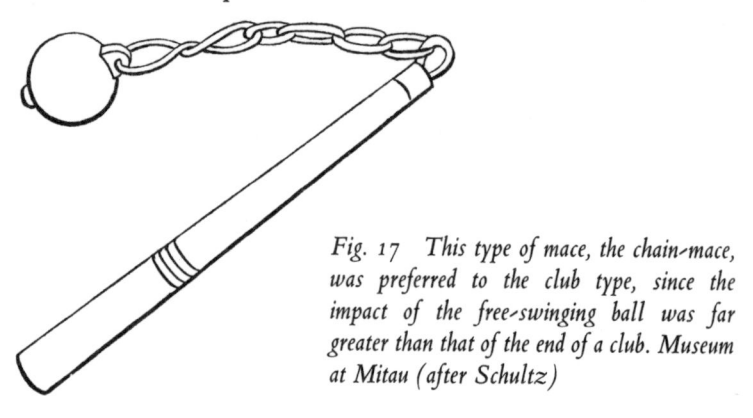

Fig. 17 This type of mace, the chain-mace, was preferred to the club type, since the impact of the free-swinging ball was far greater than that of the end of a club. Museum at Mitau (after Schultz)

A reaction against these policies of the Salians soon made itself felt. Complaints on the part of the nobility about the king's surrounding himself with 'vilissimi homines', the *ministeriales*, grew louder. At the same time, the nobility, as a class, grew in strength. The absence of a rigid and all-embracing feudal hierarchy in Germany left the freeholder, whether noble or peasant, subject to no one but the king. The king, however, had no way of exercising effective control over the free nobility as a whole. The nobles gradually extended their powers over the free peasant population on their estates in analogy to the extension of the counts' powers over the free peasantry on the domains of the Crown. Simultaneously, the nobility sought to strengthen its economic position through monastic foundations and the revenues they yielded. Most of these monasteries remained dependent on their noble founders rather than becoming dependencies of the Crown. Nominally, of course, they were subject to the papacy. The German Church, in short, was split into two parts: one part subject to the king, the other to its noble founders.

In 1070 the Saxon and Thuringian peasantry, led by the able Otto of Nordheim and Magnus Billung, revolted. Henry, however, supported by the greater part of the episcopate as well as by the dukes of Lower Lorraine, Bavaria, and Swabia, was able to crush the Saxons without difficulty. The leaders of the revolt were imprisoned and the fortifications in Thuringia increased. In 1073 a second revolt by the free Saxon peasantry as well as the Saxon nobility, again led by Otto of Nordheim, broke out. Differences in the objectives of the two factions—reduction of royal exactions on the one hand, displacement of the *ministeriales* at court on the other—proved to be a divisive factor of which Henry was able to take full advantage. Finally, at the battle of Homburg on the Unstrut in June 1075, the Saxon nobility, with an army of serfs, was defeated by Henry, the noble leaders deprived of their fiefs, and Saxony and Thuringia pillaged. Otto of Nordheim, released from prison by the end of the year, was appointed viceroy—presaging, perhaps, an intention on the part of Henry to settle the Saxon problem by governing Saxony through royal *ministeriales*.

But far greater problems now confronted Henry. In 1073 Gregory VII was elected to the Holy See. Two years later, intending to reform the relationship of the Church to society, he promulgated the *Dictatus papae*, consisting of the following twenty-seven propositions:[3]

1. That the Roman Church was founded solely by God.
2. That only the Roman Pontiff can by right be called universal.
3. That only he can depose and reinvest bishops.
4. That his legate ought to take precedence over all bishops in a council, and can pronounce sentence of deposition against them, even if he be of lower rank.
5. That the Pope can depose those absent from a council.
6. That, among other matters, one ought not to remain in the same house with those excommunicated by him.
7. That he alone has the right to issue new laws, assemble new congregations...
8. That he alone has the right to use the imperial insignia.
9. That all princes are to kiss the feet of the Pope alone.

10. That only his name is to be recited in churches.
11. That his name is unique.
12. That he ought to have the right to depose emperors.
13. That he ought to have the right to transfer bishops...
14. That he can ordain a clerk from any church...
15. That he who is ordained by him can preside over another church but cannot serve it in an inferior capacity...
16. That no synod should be called general without his command.
17. That no chapter or book should be regarded as canonical without his order.
18. That his sentence cannot be retracted by anyone...
19. That he ought not to be judged by anyone.
20. That no one should dare to condemn an appellant to the Apostolic Throne.
21. That the more important cases of every church ought to be referred to the Holy See.
22. That the Roman Church has never erred, nor, in accordance with Scripture, will ever err, in all eternity.
23. That the Roman Pontiff has without doubt been sanctified by the merits of the blessed Peter if he was canonically ordained...
24. That at his command and with his permission subordinates can bring accusations against superiors.
25. That he can depose or reinstate bishops without a synod.
26. That he who disagrees with the Church of Rome be not considered a Catholic.
27. That he can release vassals from allegiance to evil men.

The ensuing struggle between empire and papacy is known as the Investiture Contest.

Far more, however, was involved than the problem of lay investiture, which, in fact, was a negotiable matter to both parties. One of the main issues was the principle of canonical election to ecclesiastical office, which would make it impossible

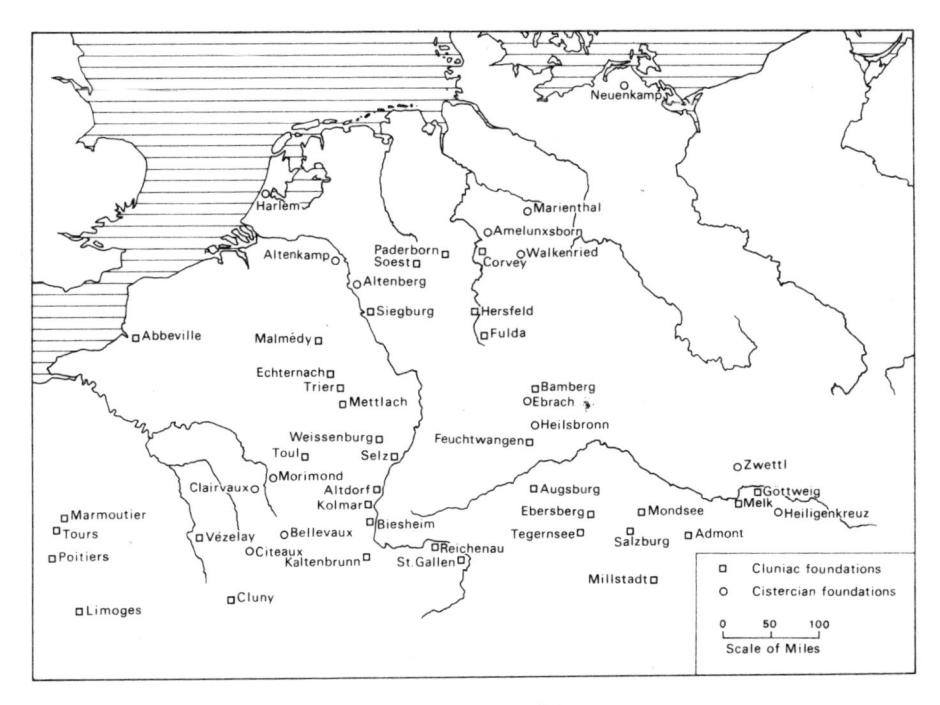

Fig. 18   Cluniac reform and the Cistercians in Central Europe

for the king to exert influence on the electors. Insistence on this principle endangered royal policy and challenged the king's position as *rex et sacerdos*. Conversely, the concept of a sacerdotal kingship was a constant source of danger to a reforming papacy, intent on tightening ecclesiastical discipline and asserting absolute authority over the Church. Therefore the person of the king was viewed by Gregory as dispensable if, in the Pope's opinion, he ceased to fulfil his function as a just king and became an 'evil man'.

The conflict between empire and papacy, flaring into civil war, wrought havoc with the fabric of German society and brought about a re-alignment of political forces. The Cluniac reform movement, which originated at the monastery of Cluny during the preceding century and had, as one of its aims, the termination of control of the nobility over churches, was not

Fig. 18

anti-imperial in itself. Its enemy was the nobility which exploited monastic foundations; its ally and protector, the king. The Cluniac monastic organization, however, was of immense usefulness to the papacy in its attempt to establish papal supremacy over the episcopate. The control which the abbot of Cluny retained over all affiliated monastic foundations assured maximum cohesiveness among the member cloisters of the cluniac monastic network, and added to its effectiveness as an instrument of propaganda for papal supremacy within the Church. Moreover, Cluny and its network of affiliates were totally autonomous, save for the authority of the Pope. Ironically enough this dependance on the papacy led to the alliance of the Cluniac movement, of which the monastery of Hirsau was the pre-eminent German foundation, with its opponent, the nobility. The nobility found it a useful tool with which to counter royal policy.

By February 1075 the initial conciliatory negotiations between Henry and the Pope had broken down: the Pope prohibited lay investiture. As soon as Henry had defeated the Saxons, he moved against the Pope by supporting the cause of the German bishops against papal supremacy, and by backing his candidate for the bishopric of Milan by force of arms against the papal candidate. On December 8, 1075, the Pope demanded the king's penance and threatened him with deposition. Henry, backed by his bishops, replied, justifying his theocratic position as follows:[4]

> 'Henry, king not by usurpation but by the sacred ordination of God, to Hildebrand, presently not pope, but a false monk.
> 'You have deserved a greeting such as this by your disturbances, since there is no rank in the Church which you have not made participate in confusion rather than honour, in malediction rather than benediction. To mention a few select cases out of many, not only have you not hesitated to lay hands upon the rulers of the Holy Church, the anointed

of the Lord—archbishops, bishops, and priests—but you have trodden them under foot as if they were slaves who did not know what their master was about.... We have endured all this, eager to preserve the honour of the Apostolic See; you, however, have taken our humility to be fear, have not hesitated to challenge the royal power conferred on us by God, and have dared threaten to divest us of it: as if we had received our realm from you, as if kingdom and empire were in your hand rather than that of God! And this despite the fact that our Lord Jesus Christ called us to the kingdom, but did not call you to the priesthood. For you rose by the following steps: through wiles, abhorred by the monk's profession, you have amassed money; with money, favour; with favour, the sword; with the sword, the throne of peace; and from the throne of peace you have disturbed the peace in arming subjects against their rulers, in teaching—you, who were not called—that our bishops called by God are to be spurned, in usurping for laymen the ministry over their priests and permitting them to depose or condemn those whom they themselves had received as teachers from the hand of God through the laying on of hands of the bishops. Us also you have attacked, who—although unworthy—are nevertheless anointed to the kingdom, and who—as the authority of the holy Fathers teaches, declaring that we are not to be deposed for any crime save, God forbid, straying from the Faith—are to be judged by God alone.... St Paul, not sparing an angel of heaven for preaching otherwise, has not excepted you who preach otherwise on earth. For he says: "If any one, I or an angel from Heaven, should preach a gospel other than that which has been preached to you, he shall be damned." You, therefore, damned by this curse as well as the judgment of our bishops and our own, descend and surrender the Apostolic Throne which you have usurped. Let another ascend the throne of St Peter, who shall not commit violence under the guise of religion, but shall teach the true doctrine of St Peter. We, Henry, king by the grace of God, with all our bishops, say to you: Descend, descend, and be eternally damned!'[5]

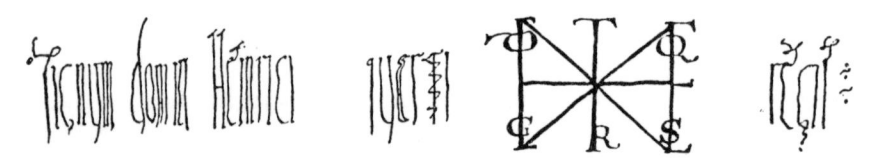

Fig. 19 Signature of Henry IV on a document from 'Leodio' (Liège) dated April 15, 1064. Legend: 'Signum domni Heinrici quarti regis'. The royal mark is constituted by the diagonals in the monogram (after Jäger)

Plate 18

Gregory thereupon excommunicated the king, and Henry, in the presence of the German bishops at Mainz, excommunicated the Pope. Gradually, however, opposition to the king grew, and the princes were able to impose their terms: withdrawal of the papal excommunication within four months or deposition of the king. Instead of abiding by the stricture of the Diet of Tribur (1076) to wait for the Pope's judgment, Henry boldly sought out the Pope at Canossa, whence Gregory, on his way to Germany, had withdrawn on hearing of the king's approach. Henry appeared at the castle gate for three consecutive days in the hairshirt of the penitent before the Pope saw himself forced to admit and absolve him. The 'shame of Canossa', as this incident was called in the more demotic of German histories, was a diplomatic victory for the king. It not only put the Pope into a position in which he was forced to grant him absolution, but it also created a rift between the Pope and the princes, who favoured the deposition of Henry at all costs.

The king could now be deposed only by means of the election of an anti-king, an act which would lack papal support. When in March 1077, the princes elected the Swabian Rudolf of Rheinfelden, the Pope urged them first to desist from such an act

The Saxon and Salian Dynasties

for the time being, then tried to mediate between the royalists and the princes—a position which significantly lowered the prestige of the papacy, and raised that of the king. When Gregory again excommunicated Henry in 1080, and Rudolf's cause, after the indecisive battles of Mellrichstadt and Flarchheim, began to suffer from the consequences of his depredations of Church properties in an effort to replenish his resources, Henry was widely regarded as much maligned. Finally, at the battle of Hohen-Mölsen, Rudolf, though victorious, was mortally wounded and died the following night. The princes chose Hermann of Luxemburg, inept and useless, as anti-king. While Frederick of Hohenstaufen, Duke of Swabia and son-in-law of Henry, carried on the royal cause against the disintegrating opposition, Henry turned his attention to Italy.

In 1085 Hermann of Luxemburg fled to Denmark and Gregory VII died. The former was replaced, in 1088, by Eckbert of Meissen, who died two years later. With his death the opposition to the king, which had been suffering for years from discord among its members, inept leadership, and the opposition of a war-weary populace, finally crumbled. Since 1080 and Gregory's backing of the anti-king Rudolf, Henry had supported the anti-pope Clement III, from whom he received the imperial crown

Fig. 20 Silver coin of Duisburg, bearing the profile of Henry IV with crozier, a motif undoubtedly inspired by the Investiture Contest (after Jäger) 2:1

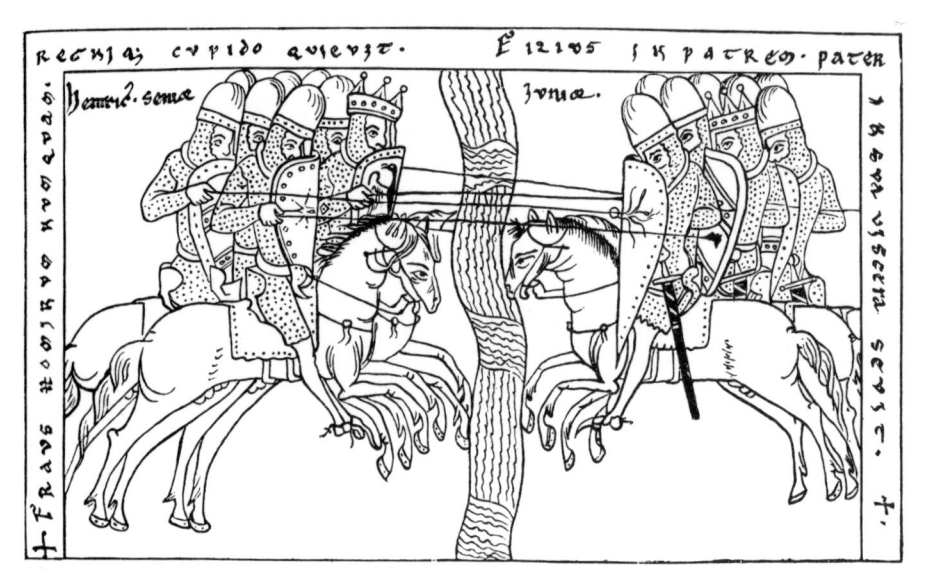

Fig. 21   Battle between Henry IV and his son on the Regen. From the Chronicle of Otto of Freising *(after* Chronik, *ed. Lammers)*

Fig. 21

in 1084. In 1088, however, the fortunes of the 'reform' party, the Gregorians, improved with the election of Urban II to the papacy. The new Pope promptly renewed the sentence of excommunication against Henry, prohibited lay investiture as well as episcopal fealty to laymen, and thus deepened the rift between Church and State by binding the episcopate exclusively to the papacy.

Henry's stubborn support of Clement III now came increasingly to be regarded as the principal obstacle to peace. Even his son Conrad became an adherent of Urban. Finally, in 1104, his second son, Henry, revolted and, claiming that his sole desire was to move his father to make peace with the Pope, gathered the dissatisfied nobility around him. In August 1105 the armies of father and son confronted each other across the river Regen, but Henry IV left the field and his army disbanded. A year later Henry IV died.

Fig. 22 Royal seal of Henry IV. Legend: 'Heinricus D(e)i Gra(tia) Rex' (after Jäger). Actual size

His alliance with the princes enabled Henry V to confront the papacy with a united Germany. Since a number of embassies to and from the Pope were able to settle nothing, Henry descended into Italy with 30,000 men. Pope Paschal II suggested an agreement, according to which the king would renounce his right of investiture and the Church return to the Crown all properties which it had acquired since the reign of Charlemagne. Henry confirmed the treaty, but Paschal was forced to withdraw it by the protests of prelates who stood to lose their fiefs. Henry thereupon took the Pope prisoner and extracted from him the right of investiture. The resulting protests of the episcopate led the Pope to revoke this privilege in 1116, without, however, excommunicating the king.

Henry's attempts to put his house in order by the resumption of vacant fiefs, the restoration of crown lands, and by increasing his reliance on the growing cities, led to the breakdown of the alliance between monarch and princes. Saxony and Frisia revolted, and by 1115 the insurrection of the princes had engulfed Lorraine, Westphalia, and Thuringia. In February of that year the royal army under the most capable of the king's *ministeriales*, the count Hoier of Mansfeld, was defeated near Welfesholz.

It is indicative of the fanaticism rampant during those years of civil war, that the Bishop of Halberstadt refused burial to the fallen of the king's army.

Upon receiving the news of the death of Pope Gregory's former ally, Mathilda of Tuscany, Henry, this time without an army, went to Italy in 1116, to take possession of Mathilda's lands. Mathilda had replaced the Holy See with Henry as beneficiary on his previous journey to Italy in 1110. In vain Henry sought an opportunity to meet with Paschal II, who was afraid of a recurrence of the events of 1111. Upon the death of Paschal in 1118 and the election of Gelasius II to the papacy, Henry caused an anti-pope, Gregory VIII, to be elected, and was, of course, promptly excommunicated. Gelasius died in the following year. Calixtus II, formerly archbishop Guido of Vienne, who now ascended the papal throne, had excommunicated Henry in 1112, and now immediately renewed the sentence. The schism within the Church was now complete. Anathema was countered by anathema, while large areas of Germany suffered daily upheavals caused by civil war and all manner of social disorder. A synod, held at Rheims in 1119, convinced the Pope, and signs of unrest of dangerous proportions among the princes prompted the king, to seek an acceptable way out of the dilemma. In order to avoid a debacle such as that which overtook the reign of his father in 1076, Henry submitted to the counsels of the princes, who now decided the imperial policy to be followed in respect to the Church. Finally, at a council at Worms on September 23, 1122, Church and State reached an agreement: the Concordat of Worms. The king renounced investiture with ring and staff, and agreed to permit canonical elections, which, however, were to take place in his presence, or that of his representative. Only after such election was the king to bestow the sceptre as symbol for investiture with secular regalia. A declaration of general amnesty to the adherents of both sides did much to bring about an atmosphere of peace and satisfaction.

Both Church and State had clearly been forced to retreat from their initial positions. One result of this was the replacement of the strength of the monarchy by the increased power of the princes. Since 1076 the nobility had steadily increased its hold over the population by subjecting great numbers of freemen to vassalage during the civil wars in the absence of effective royal authority. In the spread of feudalism, Germany now began to catch up with developments in France during the previous two centuries. The country bristled with castles, which no longer held royal garrisons, but served instead as strongpoints for the nobility and as centres for political and social organization. The weaker bound themselves in vassalage to the stronger, while the weakest sank to serfdom. Ironically, it was precisely this rise of the nobility in political power and social significance, which contributed to the rapid social ascent of the *ministeriales*. New techniques of warfare, utilizing great numbers of trained, heavily armed horsemen, rendered the lightly armed peasant foot-soldier useless. As it became increasingly necessary to man castles with trained, armed men, and to staff increasingly complex households and administrations with officials, the demand for *ministeriales* rose sharply. The *ministeriales* themselves were not slow to take advantage of this situation by shedding their personal bondage, converting their tenures into fiefs, and making their entry into the lower ranks of the nobility.

The shift of power from the monarchy to the princes became evident after the death of Henry V (1125), who, in the absence of direct heirs, designated his nephew Frederick of Swabia as his successor. The princes, however, under the leadership of Archbishop Adalbert of Mainz, elected Lothar of Supplinburg, duke of Saxony, the victor at the battle of Welfesholz. By this act, the tradition of hereditary succession to the German Crown was broken, and election made dependent on the willingness of the candidate to abide by the strictures imposed by the princes. Among the rights which Lothar surrendered were two granted

Fig. 23 Signature of Lothar of Saxony on a deed from Neuss, dated May 2, 1131. Beginning with Lothar's signature, no royal mark is ascertainable (after Jäger)

by the Concordat of Worms: the requirement that canonical elections be held in the king's presence or that of his representative, and that ecclesiastics render him homage. When, moreover, Lothar went to Rome in 1132, he recognized the papal claim to the inheritance of the lands of the countess Mathilda of Tuscany, accepted them as a fief from Innocent II, and thereby put himself in the position of vassal to the papacy. Lothar's reign—all but five years of which was occupied by a war against the Hohenstaufen and their anti-king Conrad—did nothing to impair the power of the princes. Judging by contemporary accounts, however, he seems to have enjoyed considerable popularity.[6]

The occurrences of 1125 repeated themselves after Lothar's death in 1138. Lothar had sent the royal insignia to his son-in-law, Henry the Proud, duke of Bavaria and Saxony, designating him as his successor. But even Henry, unquestionably the most powerful vassal in Germany, could not command the votes of the princes and the clerical party, headed by the archbishop of Trier. The hereditary principle was dealt another blow by the election of the former anti-king, Conrad III. Conrad's reign was plagued by the opposition of the powerful Bavarian dynasty of the Welfs. Again anarchy prevailed in large parts of Germany, and the monarchy lost what little prestige it still had after the reign of Lothar. The particularism of the princes, succeeding the centralizing tendencies of the royal administration, undid the achievements of administrative consolidation by the Crown. The prestige of the German monarchy had reached its lowest ebb.

These trends—first the shift of power from the nobility to the monarchy, then the consolidation of royal power and its eventual dissipation—found their expression in the arts. The exercise of Carolingian techniques in architecture and art was impaired by the Norman invasions of France and by the Hungarian inroads into northern Italy. Even as late as 1050 the abbey of St Martin des Champs in Paris, as well as the cathedral in St Etienne stood in ruins. Structures such as the abbey built in Aurillac around 900 and the second church at Cluny attest to a considerable decline in technical skill. It was here, in France and Lombardy, that a revitalization, a veritable fever of building and rebuilding, began shortly after the year 1000 and that the Romanesque style was developed. From here it spread, in its second phase, to the rest of Europe.

In Germany, however, the influence of Carolingian arts remained effective. Toward the end of the ninth century, while the monastic workshops of St Denis, Tours, and Corbie declined, German centres survived and gradually took their place. Charlemagne's palace chapel at Aachen served as a symbol of imperial power and was a model for similar structures at Nijmegen, Liège, Ottmarsheim, and Essen. In the construction of new churches and cathedrals, the east and west ends were given equal emphasis, in keeping with Carolingian tradition. The centres of artistic activity during the Ottonian period were the cathedral schools and Benedictine monasteries, such as Reichenau, Trier, Hildesheim, Regensburg, and Fulda, which, of course, did not remain unaffected by the political alliance of Church and State, since they did not lack connection with noble

Figs. 3, 4

families. The relationship of Ottonian to Carolingian art can, in fact, be characterized in similar terms as the political relationship of the two periods: while the Carolingian empire served as monarchic ideal for Ottonian rule, it was not the only basis on which that rule rested. Just so, Carolingian art forms one, but not the sole basis for the development of Ottonian art. The latter cannot simply be explained in terms of a development from the former, since it also derives impetus from late Roman art without the mediation of Carolingian art.

As national interests gradually asserted themselves in politics, uniquely German stylistic developments in architecture and the arts appeared. A case in point is provided by the various forms of capitals. Magdeburg cathedral, begun in 955 and destroyed by fire in 1208, was reminiscent, in its architectural form as well as in the use of the most precious building materials, of Carolingian court architecture. The composite capital is an example of the quasi-antique Carolingian style of decoration of the interior. The church of St Cyriacus at Gernrode, built by the margrave Gero c. 961, is almost devoid of Carolingian forms. The capitals are not of the quasi-antique types common to the Carolingian period, but trapezoid or floral capitals, suggesting Byzantine influence. Of particular significance here, however, is the simplicity of the

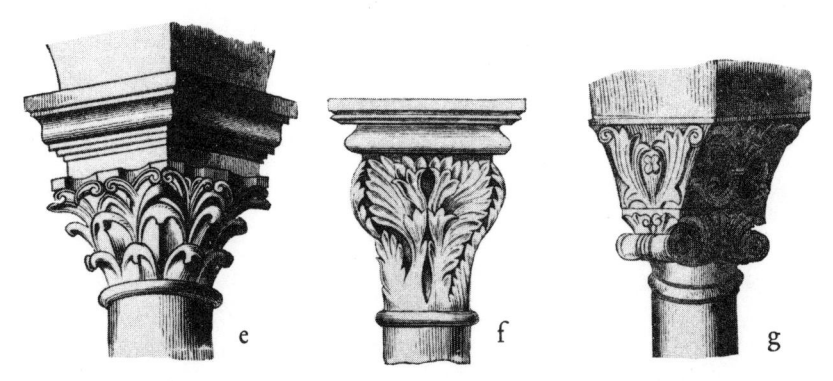

Fig. 24 Romanesque capitals: a, cuboid, St Michael's, Hildesheim; b–g, leaf capitals (after Kraus)

structure as a whole, as well as the clarity of the relationship between its parts. Most important, and foreshadowing Romanesque developments, is the effect achieved by an axial organization of space. The four arches of the arcades, for instance, rest upon a sequence of pillar, column, pillar, column, pillar. The central pillar divides this sequence into twice two supports. Similarly, a central pillar divides the twelve openings in the galleries above the aisles into twice six. The entire set is divided into six supporting arches, each of which encompasses two of the openings, yielding a series of twice three times two. As a result of this type of grouping, space and its delimitations seem static: the wall no longer 'runs', but 'stands', and each segment of the ground plan likewise maintains its own static identity.

Shortly after the year 1000 work was begun on St Michael's in Hildesheim under Bishop Bernward. Everything in this church was reduced to its basic form, and the capitals, which did not escape this simplification, show a complete break with antique tradition. The antique floral capital, however simplified or generalized, was replaced by a stark new abstract form, that of the cuboid capital, with its rounded surfaces descending toward the shaft of the pillar. This transition from cylindrical pillar to the square basis of the arch is unique. Similarly, the treatment of the

Fig. 24a

walls in colour avoids all suggestion of depth, of tectonic values, and thus reinforces the abstract quality, thereby emphasizing the affinity of the supporting pillars and their cuboid capitals with the walls. Each individual item, each individual form, whether cuboid capital or unrelieved wall surface is subordinated to the over-all concept of the abstract.

A similar structural tendency is observable in the realm of sculpture and depictions in relief. Again one must turn to Bishop Bernward's church of St Michael's, to its bronze doors, which were later moved to the cathedral of Hildesheim. The bronze doors of the Carolingian period, such as those in the chapel at Aachen, show late classical influence in the balanced relationship of frame and content. The Hildesheim doors reflect nothing of this influence. The frames of the sixteen fields are not emphasized as separate entities from the fields within; even the broad horizontal strip in the middle does not assert itself as fulfilling a divisive function. The lions' heads with rings are attached quite haphazardly, covering partly the frame, partly the field. In short, Bernward's doors are designed as a pictorial strip, rather than as a series of isolated pictures. The arrangement of the pictures bears this out. On the left side are eight scenes, tracing, from top to bottom, the development of sin from the creation of Adam to the murder of Abel. On the right side, to be read from bottom to top, is the story of salvation from the Annunciation to the Resurrection. In short, each part is structurally subordinated to the composition as a whole.

It is in manuscript illustration and decoration, however, that the artistic achievements of the Ottonian period are most clearly recognizable. The most important innovation, the pictorial presentation of the story of the New Testament, was made in the monastery of Reichenau. Episodes of the life of Christ were no longer rendered as isolated scenes, but were now the subject of pictorial series. For example, the Codex Egberti—written for archbishop Egbert of Trier about 980—consists of fifty-one

Fig. 25 Parable of the toilers in the vineyard, from the Codex Aureus, Echternach, *c. 983–992 (Landesbibl. Gotha). The miniatures of this codex continue the lateral compositional principle of the Codex Egberti, but the strips parallel the text very closely; see also Plates 28, 30 (after Kraus)*

pictures illustrating the life of Christ from the Annunciation to the Resurrection. The pictorial representations—the gestures, clothing, and buildings—are classical. After all, the tenth-century illustrators of the life of Christ had no indigenous pictorial tradition upon which they could draw. The only sources which came into question were early Christian, i.e. late Roman or Byzantine illustrations. It seems that the model for the codex was late Roman, but all suggestion of a third dimension, everything spacially illusionistic, has disappeared. In the absence of all spacially significant objects, the figures are the vehicles of the depicted action and its significance. The reduction of spacial illusion has been noted in connection with Carolingian art. In this respect, Ottonian art—and especially clearly the Codex Egberti—goes a step further: the figures are totally independent of environment, whereby the economy and poignancy of the message are increased. Comparison of the Egbert Codex with another product of Reichenau, the Aachen Otto Codex, reveals a further development of Ottonian manuscript illumination. The composition of the illustrations in the Codex Egberti is lateral, that

Plates 22–24

Fig. 25

71

of those in the Otto Codex is vertical, covering the entire page. The Otto Codex also uses Carolingian architectonic frames— Carolingian, that is, except for the fact that here they appear more like a Romanesque housing, into which the painting is fitted with its own frame. This effect of monumentality, of a grand festiveness, is enhanced by the technique of using a gilt ground in paintings—a technique which, in Western Europe, was first applied at Reichenau.

The Gospel of Otto III, another product of Reichenau, represents a further development. The figures no longer form a closed unit against an architectural background as in the Aachen Otto Codex. The most important figure of a group, such as that of Christ in the depiction of the washing of the feet, or of Otto III enthroned, clearly dominates the picture, while all the rest are subordinated in gradation to it. The architectural frame no longer merely contains the group, but contributes to the visual dominance of the main figure. By this time the figure itself has completely shed all association with the three dimensions; it has, in a sense, become one-dimensional: its significance now lies in its function, and its function is embodied by a gesture. The figure exists for the sake of the gesture which conveys its 'meaning'.

The power and significance of the Saxon dynasty found its expression in numerous depictions of the emperors, of which that of Otto III is perhaps the most noteworthy. It consists of two parts: on the left-hand page, reading from right to left, Roma, Gallia, Germania, and Sclavinia, render homage and bear gifts: on the right-hand page the enthroned emperor is flanked on his left by two warriors, on his right by two clerics. Here and in other pictures of this type, we find nothing that would distinguish the emperor as an individual, neither his features nor any other personal traits being delineated. Its significance lies precisely in the supra-individual, the general: the figure of the emperor serves only as the personification of Saxon imperial power and as an expression of its dignity and majesty. This depiction of the

Fig. 26   Missal of Henry II, Staatsbibl. Munich (after Middleton)

emperor, with the staff in his right hand, and the orb in his left, also appears on contemporary imperial seals and remains standard for centuries.

Perhaps the best example of the goldsmith's art during this period is afforded by the imperial crown, now in the Schatz, kammer in Vienna. It is composed of eight gold plates, rounded off on top, of which the four larger ones are covered with precious stones and pearls, while the other four bear figures. A cross, encrusted with precious stones, is mounted on the front plate and extends above it. From its base an arch bearing the inscription 'Chuonradus dei gratia Romanorum Imperator' (i.e. Conrad II), rises above the body of the crown. The political significance of the crown is expressed in the message of the depictions on the plates: the *majestas domini* with the inscription 'Per me reges regnant', while the Old Testament figures of David, Solomon, and Hezekiah exemplify royal and other virtues.

It is only natural that in those regions of Europe which had suffered most from the incursions of the Norsemen and the Magyars, a period of training had to precede a reawakening of the creative impulse: craftsmanship must precede artistry. The first Romanesque phase can, to a large extent, be characterized as a period of preparation, of re-learning what had been forgotten or fallen into disuse over a period of a hundred years. Since Germany, however, did not suffer the fate of France or Northern Italy, Carolingian art was able to exert its influence and serve as a basis for an unbroken tradition of artistry. The Ottonian art of Germany is contemporary with the French Romanesque of the first phase: the abbey of Limburg (1025–1042), for instance, or St Michael's at Hildesheim, with St Martin du Canigou (consecrated in 1026), or Notre Dame de la Basse Oeuvre at Beauvais. Romanesque, therefore, made its entry into Germany when in its second phase.

Before the mid-eleventh century it had been customary to cover naves and aisles of churches with timber roofs and wooden ceilings. Apart from the fact that such construction presented an ever-present fire hazard—and reports of fires destroying churches with wooden roofs are no rarity in the chronicles of the time—a

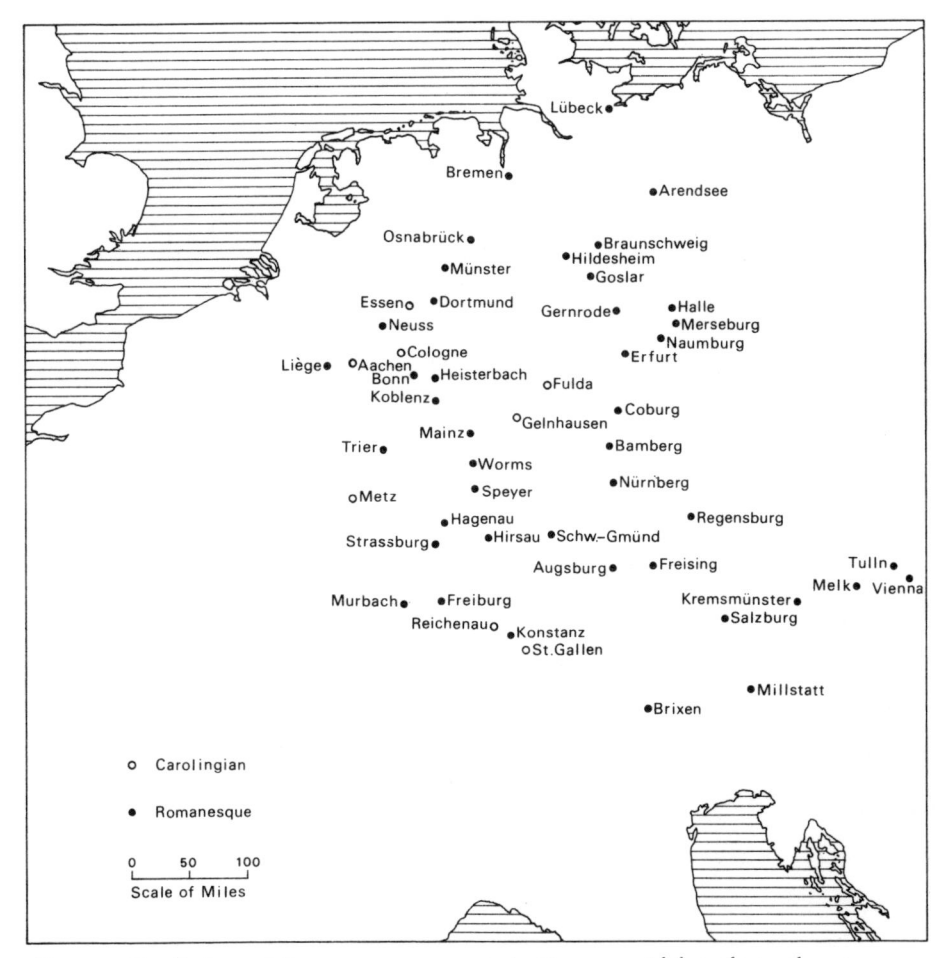

Fig. 27   Carolingian and Romanesque monuments in Germany, eighth to thirteenth century

more prosperous age, a more securely settled society demanded that the house of God, usually the only public building of a town, be stronger and more imposing than other structures. In order to meet this challenge, it was necessary to overcome the handicap of the wooden roof by vaulting the entire building in stone. This achievement, and the constant struggle with the problems created by the oblique thrust of round arch and vault upon their supports, characterize the second Romanesque phase. The necessity of controlling this thrust of the vault led to the use of compound piers, with which the ribs or transverse arches were fused in such a manner that the framework of the vault and the skeleton of the wall created a harmony, which once and for all eliminated the pre-Romanesque clash of flat wall against flat ceiling.

Plate 35

The vault over the nave of the cathedral of Speyer, which replaced a flat timber ceiling *c.* 1080, is one of the earliest examples of a large groined vault. It would, however, be misleading to regard the vaulted nave as a characteristic of Romanesque without exception. While Cluny covered the nave of its church with a barrel-vault, its German dependency, Hirsau, chose to retain the flat timber ceiling, the heavy pillar, and to dispense with a crypt and a choir at the west end. Hirsau, in short, continued a conservative trend, which took its departure from the early Christian basilica. The example of cross-vaulting at Speyer was followed in the abbey church of Königslutter. Here, however, ornamentation was not used as sparingly as elsewhere: the piers of its double-aisled cloisters are richly decorated, whereas in most German Romanesque structures of this period ornamentation is restricted to the galleries around the apses, pilaster strips, and the arched courses under the eaves. Rather than fulfilling an independent function, sculpture played an ornamental role and was generally stylized and subordinated to its architectural environment. An example of such stylization is afforded by the

Plate 33

'Adoration of the Magi' from the doors of Sta Maria im Kapitol at Cologne (*c.* 1050). This does not mean, however, that Romanesque sculpture or carving could not be expressive: a fusion of stylization and expressiveness was achieved, for instance, in the Apostles and Prophets in the cathedral of

Plate 34

Bamberg.

It is frequently claimed that the development of vaulting inhibited the progress of wall painting. The various types of supports, pillars, pilasters, and massive compound piers necessary for the support of lateral and transverse arches, broke up wall space into small compartments unsuitable as surfaces for large murals, and the new architecture often prevented sufficient light from entering: naves with galleries, steeped in gloom, were not suitable for the display of decorative painting.

It would be a mistake, however, to assume that Romanesque churches were bare of painting. In recent years many Romanesque murals have come to light, casting considerable doubt upon the opinion that painting played no great role in churches of the period. The use of brilliant colours characterized the presentation of scenes from the Old or the New Testament, scenes the components of which testify to the increasing dominance of iconographical tradition. Architectural limitations such as arches and arcades, which break up the surface of the wall, are often used tectonically as part of the painting, as for instance in the depiction of Christ, flanked by the apostles arranged in arcades in the church at Prüfening near Regensburg. The arcade symbolizes, in this context, the Heavenly Palace, the Heavenly Jerusalem. However, the arrangement itself is clearly influenced by the traditional depiction of king or emperor. Romanesque painting, like sculpture, tended toward the schematic, making use of geometric forms in the interpretation of the human figure. Moreover, both the murals at Prüfening as well as those in the All Saints' chapel in the cathedral cloister at Regensburg clearly reflect Byzantine influence, even though they are very badly preserved. This influence on Romanesque painting, by no means limited to Germany, increased with more frequent contact with Byzantium, directly and via Italy, following the marriage of Otto II to the Byzantine princess Theophano in 972.

The massiveness of the walls and their relatively few, small windows gave Romanesque churches an appearance of heavy solidity, of functioning as foreign bodies in a temporal sea. In this sense, Romanesque architecture reflects the style of contemporary devoutness—monastic rather than urban, severe rather than secular. In Pseudo-Dionysian terms grown familiar through Duns Scotus' translation of *De coelesti ierarchia*, the darkness of the interior signifies the darkness of the world, in which the Eternal Light is conceivable through analogy. The pictures decorating the walls were likewise not regarded as beautiful *per se*, but as analogies to undepictable beauty. The colours were anti-naturalistic in order to emphasize their analogic function and to draw attention to the supraterrestrial nature of pictorial light. By implication, the function of the colours serves to emphasize the nature of light, rather than of phenomena, as the essence of existence—an aesthetic interpretation of Pseudo-Dionysian metaphysics.

Manuscript illumination, like mural painting, exhibits many Byzantine characteristics. In fact, miniature painting offers a far more reliable basis upon which this influence can be judged, since illuminated manuscripts from this period are more often and better preserved than mural paintings. Furthermore, the fact that murals, and particularly stained glass of the twelfth century, show the profound influence of book illumination, enables one to use the latter as an example, to some degree, of currents in wall painting and the staining of glass.

Each of these arts is influenced by the dominant political issue of the period, the Investiture Contest. In the latter part of the eleventh century, for instance, the Italianate, Gregorian style of manuscript illumination and wall painting in the area around Salzburg, Tegernsee, and Freising, is to be distinguished from the 'imperial' style of the so-called Bavarian school of painting, which adheres to Carolingian and Ottonian models. The Bavarian school influenced pro-imperial Bohemia, and it is here that one of the clearest examples of this stylistic tendency is to be found in the Coronation Gospels at Prague.[7]

Around the turn of the century, a reaction against the occasionally extreme stylization in manuscript illumination of the previous

Fig. 28 Illustration from the legend of St Thomas, in the Passiones Apostolorum (Staatsbibl. Munich) about 1150, depicting the lion's dismemberment of the attendant who had struck St Thomas at a banquet. The attendant meets his punishment while fetching water. Note the limitation of the depiction to the objects necessary for an understanding of the story. The picture is to be 'read' (after Hauttmann)

quarter of a century set in. Figures are endowed with a new freshness and unstylized facial expressions. Simultaneously, however, a trend toward monumentality and severity of expression asserted itself. Figures are often disposed in geometric patterns on the picture surface and tend to serve a primarily ornamental function. Outlines become emphasized, and serve not only as delimitations of the depicted forms, but display an independent ornamental value. The qualities of painting are played down, those of drawing become even more obvious.

Plates 36, 37
Plate 39

Plate 40

Plates 41–43

Neoplatonic ideas, particularly those of the Pseudo-Areopagite, were expressed not only in Ottonian and Romanesque art and architecture, but also in the theory of music. Otloh, monk of St Emmeram (*c.* 1010–1070) and author of the most comprehensive treatise of Romanesque aesthetics—the *Dialogus de tribus quaestionibus*—regards harmony as the common characteristic of all Creation: the *convenientia rerum dissimilium*. Consequently, harmony or its analogies form the necessary basis for all arts. Absalom, abbot of Springiersbach near Trier (*fl. c.* 1200), follows Otloh and Guido of Arezzo (*c.* 990–1050) in regarding harmony as a basic characteristic of the universe. His *Sermo XX in Annuntiatione Beatae Mariae* is a summary statement of medieval neoplatonic aesthetics. Absalom distinguishes between a *musica animalis*, analogous to the harmony of the five senses and corresponding to the *diapente*, a *musica spiritualis*, signifying the harmony of the four cardinal virtues and expressed allegorically by the *diatessaron,* and a *musica coelestis*, symbolizing eternal joy after the resurrection by the *diapason*.

The traditional treatment of German literature of the Ottonian period illustrates the danger of a facile use of the term 'renaissance'. The so-called Ottonian renaissance in literature consisted of three principal components: the Latin heroic epic, *Waltharius manu fortis*, once ascribed to Ekkehart I of St Gallen, the Latin beast epic *Ecbasis captivi*, and the Latin works of the nun Roswitha of Gandersheim. Current research ascribes the *Waltharius* to the late Carolingian period. The *Ecbasis captivi*, an allegorical poem about the misadventures of a calf which had strayed from the stall, i.e. the dangers of escape from monastic discipline, can probably be ascribed to the eleventh century. Only Roswitha remains—scarcely sufficient to support any notion of a 'renaissance'. Her strictly literary significance, resting mainly on her adaptations of some plays of Terence to the demands of Christian moralization, is limited: her attempts at the use of dialogue— one hesitates to employ the term 'drama'—found no imitators. Of greater significance in the larger context of contemporary eulogistic accounts of the deeds of the emperors was her *De gestis Oddonis I imperatoris* in hexameters. It was to be expected that the power and prestige of the Ottonian monarchy would bring about an increase in the production of such eulogies, some of which rise above the level of mere effusions of encomia and are valuable historical works. Among the most notable historians of the period were Liutprand, the ambassador of Otto I to the Pope and to Byzantium, who undertook to write a history of Europe from 888 to his own time, and Widukind, monk of Corvey and author of a history of the Saxons.

As far as literature in the narrower sense is concerned, the letters of Froumund (c. 960–1008), composed for use as stylistic models, and especially his poems, reflect some of the secular spirit usually associated with the succeeding generation. Of particular note is the panegyrical *Modus Ottinc* in praise of the Ottos, the oldest dateable *modus*, i.e. one of a genre of nonstrophic rhythmic forms descended from the sequence. The sequence is an Alleluja trope, which, according to Notker Balbulus, was made necessary by the problem of remembering the *jubilus*, the melisma adorning the final vowel of the Alleluja in the Mass.[8] In the collection that contains the *Modus Ottinc*, the so-called Cambridge Songs, there is also the panegyrical macaronic poem *De Heinrico*, in which alternating Latin and German lines rhyme—a form that recurs later in the poetry of the *vagantes*, the wandering scholars.

Literature in the German language during the Ottonian period is practically non-existent. Of significance, however, are the translations by Notker Labeo (c. 950–1022) of some works of Aristotle, Boethius' *Consolation of Philosophy* and of the allegorical *Marriage of Mercury and Philology* by Martianus Capella, which was one of the basic texts in the *trivium*. These translations, with interspersed commentary, had an exclusively pedagogical purpose, but they do reveal Notker's genius in rendering technical terms for which no German equivalents existed, as well as his sensitivity for phonetic characteristics, which enabled him to develop his own orthographic system.

In the period of the first Salian kings, as in the Ottonian period, not much literature in the German language was produced. The court of Henry III seems to have attracted a number of scholars, among them the chaplain Wipo, author of a history of Conrad II, didactic verse, and the Easter sequence *Victimae paschalis*. Some of the anecdotal *modi* contained in the 'Cambridge Songs' originated in this period. In fact, the ancestor of this collection is probably to be associated with the reign of Henry III, who was personally interested in collecting *modi*. The middle of the century saw the composition of *Ruodlieb*, an epic poem in hexameters, astonishing in its use of courtly motifs and kaleidoscopic treatment of courtly life with its consciously regulated and disciplined forms. It is transmitted only in fragments, but its content emerges quite clearly: it is the story of a young knight seeking his fortune in the service of a great king, whose conflict with a lesser king he brings to a successful close. Richly rewarded, he returns home after numerous adventures, and unmasks as a priest's mistress a young lady who had been chosen to be his wife. His mother dreams of high honours which are to befall her son, a dream which begins to come true in his obtaining the princess Heriburg with the aid of a dwarf. Beyond this point the development of the plot cannot be ascertained with certainty, but it is clear that the poet of the *Ruodlieb* makes use of themes and depicts attitudes which do not reach poetic fruition until fully a century and a half later in the Middle High German courtly literature.

As the Cluniac reform movement gathered momentum in Germany, as the issues of the Investiture Contest began to emerge ever more clearly, it was once more to the interest of all factions to appeal to the layman. It will be recalled that during the Carolingian era it had been expedient for the educated clergy to put aside its Latin learning in order to appeal in the vernacular to the lay populace of still uncertain Christian faith. Now the Cluniac call to the ascetic life, as well as the conflicting interests of emperor and Pope, likewise demanded the enlistment of popular support and sympathy, and therefore the use of the German language. After an interval of some one hundred and fifty years, German literature was again written in German.

A case in point is the *Ezzolied,* so called after its author, a canon of Bamberg. Its original version is to be dated soon after 1060, and shows no traces of the partisanship which came to characterize literary production during the conflict between empire and papacy. Approximately fifty years later, however, a second version of the *Ezzolied* made its appearance. Whereas the first or Strassburg version, as far as can be judged from the transmitted fragment, is simply a hymnic story of man's salvation, beginning with the Creation, the later or Vorau text is no longer unproblematically hymnic, but assumes a pronounced didactic character. It is also not without significance, that the older version addresses itself to 'my lords', while the popularizing Vorau *Ezzolied* calls upon 'all of you'.

The reflection of the Investiture Contest is particularly noticeable in the *Annolied* (c. 1085–1105), named after its hero Anno, archbishop of Cologne (d. 1075). An introduction which occupies 40 per cent of the poem covers both the religious and secular history of the world from the Creation to the time of Anno. The rest is a mixture of saint's 'life' and hymn. Anno was counsellor and confessor to Henry III. From 1062 to 1064 he headed the government during the minority of Henry IV and exerted great influence over the latter until his retirement from court at the end of 1072. He was an outspoken proponent of the powers claimed by the Church, and was canonized in 1183 by Pope Lucius III. But already in the *Annolied* he is regarded as a saint— possibly the first, if not the only instance in which political accomplishments in the service of the Church are made the basis for a claim to the nimbus.

The effects of the Cluniac reform are perhaps most clearly noticeable in the *Memento mori* (1070–1080) of the Hirsau monk Noggerus, later abbot of Zwiefalten. He denounces life, and stresses the evil of the world. This point of view characterizes much of German literature transmitted from the subsequent eighty years. At the end of this period it is again expressed in the *Memento mori* of Heinrich of Melk (*c.* 1160). It is a mistake, however, to conclude from the tenor of these monastic writings that all German literature produced during that time was subject to the same effects of Cluniac enthusiasm.[9] It is essential to recall that most written literature was produced by monks, reflected the monastic outlook of the time, and was preserved in monasteries. The nature of oral literature then current, and of written literature conflicting with that produced under monastic or ecclesiastical auspices and therefore far less likely to survive, is not ascertainable. There is, however, no reason to assume that it differed greatly from that of the period immediately preceding the last third of the eleventh century.

The gradual transition to the secular spirit which dominated literature throughout the courtly period is already exemplified, about 1150, by the *Alexanderlied* of the priest Lamprecht. It is scarcely more than a clumsy translation of the *Alexander* of Alberic of Besançon, and totally dependent on the early Christian Alexander-tradition, which transformed the Greek theme of Alexander's *hybris* into that of diabolic pride. Lamprecht makes use of the *memento mori* theme suggested by Alexander's early death, and underlines the message by prefacing the whole with a programmatic *vanitas, vanitatum, vanitas*. Nevertheless, between ascetic prologue and epilogue, worldly adventures unfold themselves, peopled by still unselfconscious knights. Similar evidence of a shift in emphasis from Cluniac asceticism to socially conscious secularity is provided by the artistically more impressive *Kaiserchronik*, also written about the middle of the twelfth century. Here the Augustinian notion of the historical process as twofold, embodied in *imperium* and *sacerdotum*, receives the form of a chronicle. Beginning with Caesar and the opposition of the pagan state to the early Church, the chronicle traces the relationship of these two basic components of Augustine's political theory to their reconcilement under the Emperor Constantine and Pope Sylvester. The old *imperium*, however, is conceived as ceasing with Theodosius. Significantly, the crown rests upon the altar of St Peter in Rome, until Charlemagne re-establishes the empire in union with the papacy, a union symbolized by the legendary brotherhood of Charlemagne and Pope Leo. There follows the line of German emperors, among whom Henry IV and Conrad III receive rather harsh treatment at the hands of the clerical authors. Within this framework, legendary and novelistic material—the Crescentia legend, the story of Lucrece, etc.—finds its place, endowing wordly matter, wordly deeds and heroes with an existence quite apart from Church and clergy.

There was a pause in the development of philosophical thought after the initial impetus of the Carolingian era, as there had been in intellectual life in general. The tenth and eleventh centuries, however, witnessed a resurgence of philosophical speculation not unrelated to developments in other spheres of activity. True, the sustained existence of monastic and cathedral schools as the sole centres of learning assured a continuity from the Carolingian period onward. But in the eleventh century, due to the increase in trade and the consequent rise in the importance of cities, the principal pedagogical role began to pass from the monastery schools to the cathedral schools, which now became centres of culture. Monastic schools continued to exist, continued even to be of importance, but restricted their activities primarily to the education of their monks, while their extramural functions were taken over by the cathedral schools. Here, in contrast to the monastic tradition of meditation upon sacred texts, there now developed a predominant interest in dialectics, in the sharpening of logical methods of discussion and verification of concepts and matters of faith. At this point in the history of scholasticism, it was first asserted that reason, in the form of dialectic, is competent to discuss all matters of faith. Immediately, of course, two opposing philosophical camps faced each other: the dialectitians and the anti-dialectitians. The latter, among them Manegold of Lautenbach (d. 1103) and Otloh of St Emmeram (d. 1073), maintained that reason, indeed all knowledge, was of no avail in a discussion of matters of faith, since God, being omnipotent, was above all laws and not subject even to the concept of impossibility. It is not surprising that this clash of dialectitians and anti-dialectitians —the first of several such clashes in the history of scholasticism— reached its high point during the Investiture Contest. The relationship between the assertion of the power of the Church over imperial power, ecclesiastical over secular authority, and the rejection of reason as interpreter of faith, is obvious. In Manegold of Lautenbach the standpoints of the extreme anti-dialectitian and the extreme Gregorian are united: philosophy is a temptation of the devil and to be kept in its place as handmaid of theology, the Pope is the supreme ruler on earth, and the king—just as in the *dictatus papae*—can be deposed if he is deemed by the Pope to be 'evil'.

Whereas dialectic developed and was sharpened at the cathedral schools, mysticism began to flourish in the monastery schools. The pre-eminent mystic of the period is, of course, St Bernard of Clairvaux. It was a German, however, who fashioned a philosophical basis for mysticism: Hugh of St Victor in Paris (1096–1141). The perception of nature is the basic requisite for all understanding; all experience, including the arguments of the philosophers, is potentially relevant in gaining a knowledge of God. Contemplation and faith, however, are essential. Knowledge and reason, though not to be disparaged, should serve the ends of theology. Moreover, in some of his works, notably *De sacramentis,* Hugh foreshadows the period of systematization in scholasticism, the age of the *summae,* namely the thirteenth century.

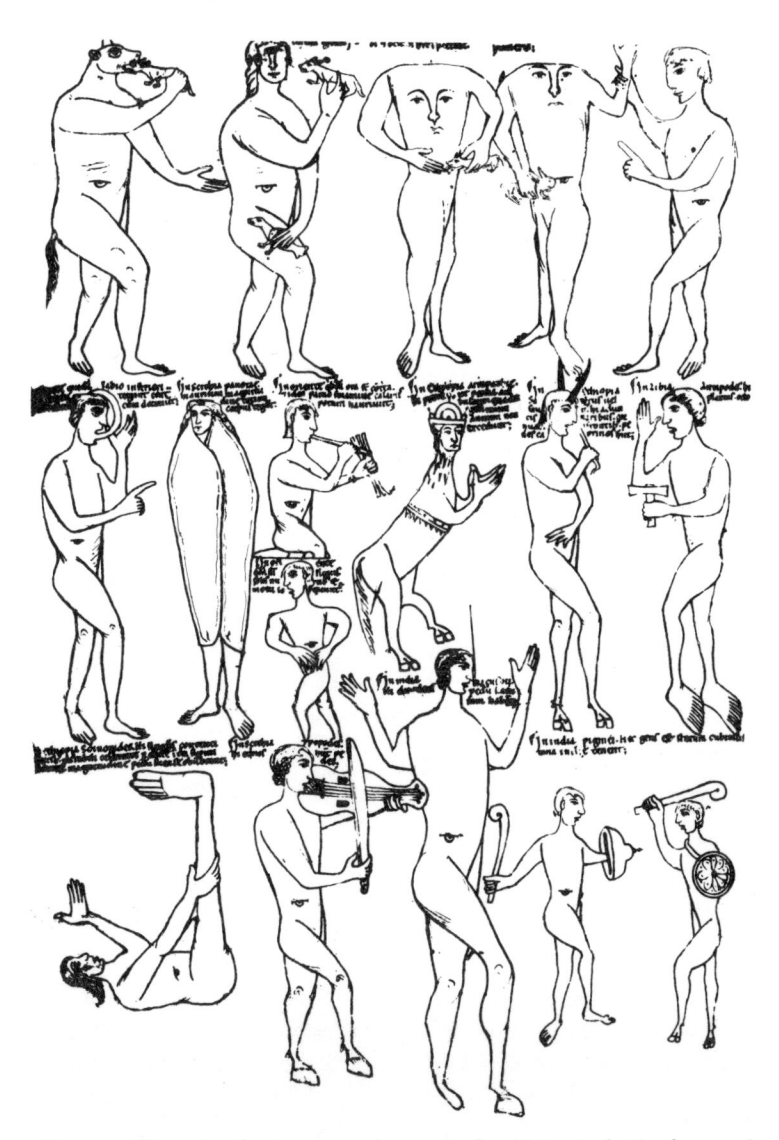

Fig. 29 Illustration from a manuscript executed at Arnstein during the second half of the twelfth century, depicting human monsters from the edges of the world, based on Solinus (third century) and Honorius Augustodunensis (twelfth century), British Museum, London. Some of these monsters play a role in the pre-courtly epic poem Herzog Ernst, *about 1170 (after Le Goff)*

Chapter III

The Chivalric Period

CONRAD DESIGNATED his nephew, Frederick of Hohenstaufen, as his successor rather than this eight-year-old son Frederick, and the princes, for a change, unanimously approved the choice. At the age of thirty, Frederick was already known for his capability of arriving at independent judgments and his determination in seeing them carried out, as well as for his eloquence. Upon the succession of Frederick I, or Barbarossa as he came to be called by the Italians, it became clear that the entire structure of the monarchy, and its relationship to both the princes and the Church, had to be redefined. The fundaments upon which the Ottonian and Salian monarchies rested were shattered once and for all. The groundwork which was to support the monarchy henceforth had to be laid anew. As far as Germany was concerned, Frederick's principal task consisted of taking advantage of the increasing density of feudal relationships, i.e. of creating a feudal state with the king at its head. The most pressing problem in the empire at large was posed by the Italian communes and their place within the political structure of the empire. Above all, it was necessary that the rights of the empire be convincingly asserted.

The most concise of such assertions was elicited by a papal embassy to Frederick at Besançon in October 1157. The apostolic legates, the cardinals Bernhard of San Clemente and Roland of San Marco, brought forth a papal letter in which there was mention of the bestowal (*collatio*) of the imperial crown, and of the fact that the Pope would have been happy if the emperor had received even greater beneficence from him. The emperor's chancellor, Reinald of Dassel, whose task it was to translate the papal message into German, rendered the word *beneficium*, which can signify either a favour or a fief, with *lêhen,* i.e. fief and *conferre*

The Chivalric Period

(*collatio*), which can mean simply 'to place (a crown) upon', with *schenken*, i.e. 'bestow upon'. Frederick thereupon issued a manifesto, in which the general reaction to the Pope's letter as well as the imperial position is made clear:

'...Truly, at that assertion, blasphemous and devoid of all truth, not only was the imperial majesty moved by righteous indignation, but also all the princes present were filled with such fury and anger, that they would doubtless have condemned those two godless priests to death, if our presence had not stayed them. Since many similar letters were found upon them, as well as sealed forms which they were to fill out afterwards in accordance with their discretion, and with which they, as had hitherto been a habit with them, intended to spray the poison of their evil over all the churches of the German empire, to plunder the altars, to carry off the vessels of the house of God and to strip the crosses, we have commanded them to return to Rome on the road on which they had come hither, so that they would have no opportunity to proceed further.

'Inasmuch as we have received the kingdom and empire by election of the princes from God alone, who, by the passion of Christ His Son, had given the governance of the earth to the two essential swords, and since the Apostle Peter taught the world "Fear God, honour the king," anyone who claims that we received the imperial crown as a benefice from the Pope, contradicts divine order as well as the teaching of Peter, and is guilty of a lie....'[1]

The effectiveness of assertions such as this was assured by the general reaction against previous discords and the widespread desire for peace and stability. But Frederick's reply was symptomatic of far more than mere defiance in the face of the papal claim. Supported by arguments from the Roman law, Frederick based his imperial claim on a secular foundation and pitted it against the theocratic arguments of the papacy. This tendency is already clearly discernible in Frederick's spirited reply to the representatives of the city and senate of Rome, who had come to meet him between Sutri and Rome in 1155 to offer him the imperial throne:

> '...You speak of the ancient renown of your city. You praise to the stars the ancient status of your sacred republic. Granted! Granted! In the words of your own author "There was, there was once virtue in this republic." Once, I say. Ò if I only could say "now" as truly as I would say it gladly. Your Rome, as also our Rome, has come to feel the vicissitudes of time.... It is well known, how first the strength of your nobility was transferred from our city here to the royal city of the East and for how many years the hungry Greeklet had sucked at the breasts of your glory. Then came the Frank, truly noble in name and kind, and divested you by force of whatever nobility remained in you. Do you want to know about the ancient glory of your Rome? The senatorial dignity? The disposition of the camp? The virtue and discipline of the equestrian order, its untarnished and unconquerable bravery in advancing into battle? Look upon our state! We have all these things. All this has descended to us, together with the empire. The empire did not come to us naked. It came garbed in its virtue, it brought along its adornments. With us are your consuls. With us is your senate. With us is your army. These leaders of the Franks shall rule you according to their counsel, these knights of the Franks shall avert harm from you with the sword. You boast that you had summoned me, that by you I had been first made a citizen, then the prince, and that I had received from you what was yours. How devoid of reason, how lacking in truth this novel assertion is, may be left to your own judgment and that of wise men! Let us consider the deeds of modern emperors and see if it was not our divine princes Charles and Otto who, by their valour and not

anyone's charity, took the City together with Italy from the Greeks and Lombards and added it to the realm of the Franks. Desiderius and Berengarius, your tyrants, teach you this, of whom you boasted and on whom you relied as your princes. From reliable sources we have learned that they were not only defeated and taken captive by our Franks, but that they grew old and died in servitude.... The power of the Franks was invoked by invitation. I would call it entreaty rather than invitation. In your misery you besought the fortunate, in your frailty the strong, in your weakness the bold, in your fear the secure. Thus invited, if one can call this an invitation, I have come. I have made your prince my vassal and until this day I have transferred you to my jurisdiction.... Let him, who is able, snatch the club from the hand of Hercules....'[2]

The canonization of Charlemagne in 1165 further aided in the sanctification of Frederick's imperialism, especially since Frederick stressed the fact that Charles won his empire by conquest, not as a gift from the Pope.

The material foundations of the monarchy had likewise to be adapted to the changed conditions. The wars of the Investiture Contest had reduced the holdings of the Crown within Germany to such a degree that it was necessary for Frederick to look beyond the boundaries of his kingdom for resources. The centres of Ottonian and Salian power, the royal domains of Saxony and Central Germany, had been laid waste. However, the seat of Hohenstaufen power, Swabia, isolated in the southwestern part of the kingdom, could become central to the empire if its location were strategically exploited to the west and south. The marriage of Frederick to Beatrice of Burgundy in 1156 was the first step in this direction, enabling him to take possession of Provence and Burgundy. The consolidation of his position in the south gave him easy access to Lombardy. Thus, from his centrally located domains, Frederick, the feudal monarch, could rule over his network of feudal dependencies. But such a rule depended on the effectiveness with which the controlling strands of this network were connected to the monarchy.

No control whatever over the nobility could be achieved without the aid of the great princes, such as Henry the Lion, duke of Saxony, the Babenberg dukes in Austria, and the ducal houses of Zähringen and Wittelsbach. Through a series of privileges, these duchies were significantly strengthened and placed, in the feudal scale, between king and nobility, while their feudal dependance on the monarchy was emphasized. In order to maintain effective recognition and acceptance of this dependence on the part of the princes, the Hohenstaufen base of power itself had to be strengthened considerably. In part, this could be accomplished by the acquisition of lands through purchase or reversion. A far quicker, more efficient way of consolidating the royal power, however, was to gain the same measure of control over Lombardy as Frederick exercised in Burgundy. The principal obstacle to the exercise of royal power in Lombardy was the power of the communes, which, in the course of time, had absorbed elements of power originally belonging to the king. It was not a matter of simple resumption of these powers on the part of the Crown, but of exacting—here as in the case of the German princes—an acknowledgment of the fact that these powers pertained to the Crown and were not held independently.

Initially, the policies which Frederick followed to that end were, on the whole, successful. The one notable exception was Milan. With the election of Alexander III to the papacy in 1159, the anti-imperial party among the cardinals triumphed, and the re-establishment of the old Gregorian alliance of the papacy with Sicily, and now also with Milan, initiated a rapid deterioration of Frederick's position in Lombardy. His attempts to reverse the course of events by force of arms ended in failure. True, in 1162 Milan was captured and sacked, but as the imperial administration of Lombardy became harsher, the Lombard communes saw

Fig. 30 Seal of Duke Henry Jasomirgott of Austria, 1150 (after Schultz)

their common interest in resistance and formed the Lombard League. After numerous attempts at negotiation and five expeditions to Italy, the imperial forces were defeated in the battle of Legnano in 1176. The eventual result was the Peace of Constance in 1183, which accorded the right of self-government to the communes. Frederick, on the other hand, emerged with considerable financial gain in return for these concessions.

What could not be achieved in Lombardy, however, could be attempted with better hope for success in Tuscany, where the development of cities lagged far behind. Here Frederick was able to establish a non-feudal, direct administration without great difficulty. In short, Frederick achieved his goal of establishing a firm, centrally administered base of power, but achieved it in central, rather than in northern Italy.

Fig. 31   Siege of a city at the time of the Hohenstaufen. From the Annals of

While Frederick was thus preoccupied with the affairs of Lombardy and Tuscany, he was forced to make concessions to the princes in Germany, among whom Henry the Lion emerged pre-eminent. Relations between Frederick and Henry the Lion became critically strained when the latter, before the battle of Legnano, informed Frederick that he would send requested reinforcements only if the emperor would reverse his decision to take Goslar, with which he had invested Henry some years before, back under his own control. His refusal to supply reinforcements was no doubt largely responsible for the defeat of Frederick at Legnano. Henry's independent attitude toward the emperor was due, in part, to his connections with the English court—he had married, in 1168, Mathilda, the daughter of Henry II—a connection which enabled him to engage in foreign policies of his own. However, any hope he may have had of enlisting the aid of the papacy against the emperor vanished with the reconciliation between Frederick and Alexander III at Venice in 1177. When Henry failed to appear on three separate occasions before a court of princes to answer for his failure to restore to the Church ecclesiastical property which he had seized, he was stripped of his two duchies Saxony and Bavaria, as well as of his fiefs. He retained only his patrimony and, banned from the realm, went to England after some resistance which was easily broken by imperial forces.

The Chivalric Period

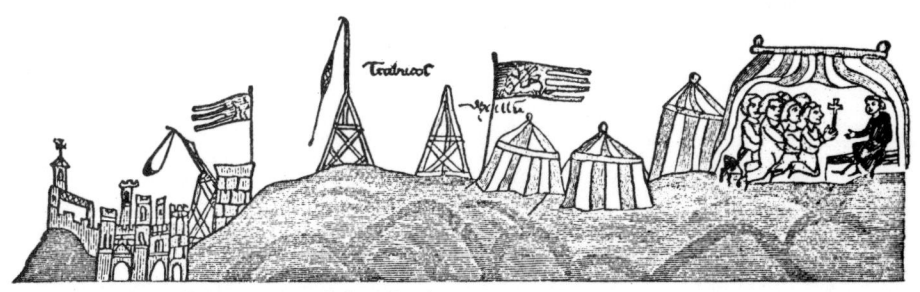

Genoa *in the Bibl. Nat., Paris (after Jäger)*

Frederick took this opportunity to fragment the basis of power for any future opposition. Saxony was divided into two parts, west and east of the Weser. The former was conferred upon archbishop Philip of Cologne as the duchy of Westphalia; the latter, the lands of Engern, was bestowed upon Bernard, the son of Albrecht the Bear. Bavaria went to Otto of Wittelsbach, but only after Styria was separated from it as a duchy held directly for the Crown by the former margrave Ottokar IV. Now royal authority extended over the length and breadth of Germany, including the northern provinces. It was feudal authority, effectively proven in feudal law, under which Henry was tried and convicted.

Fig. 32

The feudal order of German society and government was further emphasized by the creation, in 1180, of a new rank, the *Reichsfürsten*, tenants-in-chief, who stood between monarch and lesser nobility and held special privileges. The princes now, with the king at their head, were able to overcome the obstruction of the petty nobility and reconstruct the governments of their territories systematically along feudal lines. Yet these same bases of Frederick's power, the fragmentation and redistribution of the lands of Henry the Lion and the creation of the *Reichsfürsten*, led to the eventual erosion of the power for which they served as foundations. The holdings of Henry were not added to the crown lands, but returned to the nobility; and the *Reichsfürsten,* by

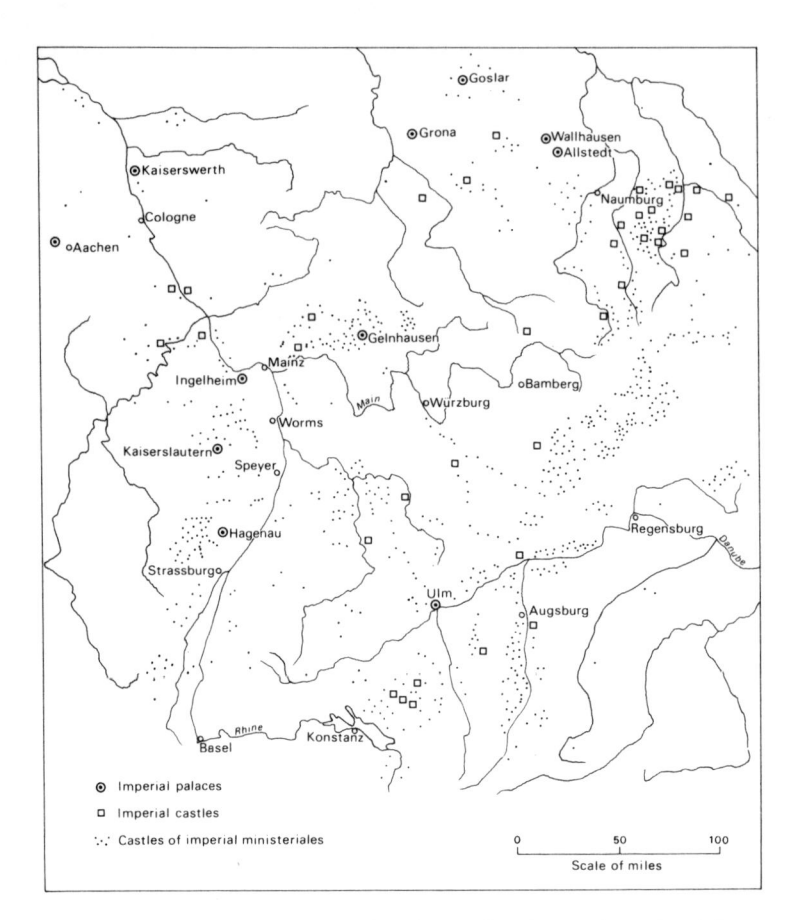

Fig. 32. Imperial palaces, imperial castles, castles of imperial ministeriales *in the Hohenstaufen period*

retaining the power of decision on the admittance of others to their rank, put themselves, rather than the king, in the position of making these crucial appointments.

For the time being, however, internal affairs seemed sufficiently stable for Frederick to entrust the kingdom to his son Henry and to participate in the third crusade. Like the second crusade, the undertaking was headed by the great European monarchs:

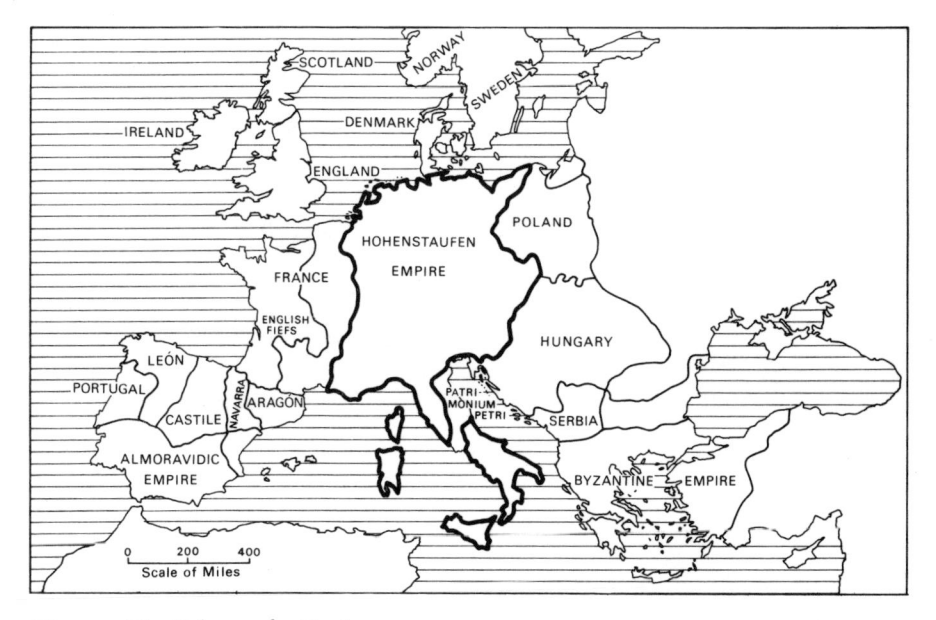

Fig. 33   The Hohenstaufen Empire

besides Frederick, Richard I of England and Philip Augustus of France took part in the venture to erase the disaster of the previous crusade and reconquer Jerusalem, which had fallen in 1187. The most grievous mistake made in connection with the first and second crusades—the accompaniment of the army by all sorts of rabble—was avoided by making the possession of three marks of silver a condition of participation. Under the guidance of Frederick and his younger son, duke Frederick of Swabia, progress through the Balkans and Greece into Asia Minor was relatively orderly and, on the whole, successful. Here, however, the death of Frederick Barbarossa by drowning (1190) led to a partial dissolution of the army; duke Frederick led the remnant to Acre.

Imperial policy took an entirely new turn with the accession of Henry VI. Upon the death of William II of Sicily in 1189, Henry, as husband of Constance of Sicily, laid claim to the Sicilian crown. The claim to Sicily was accompanied by the desire for domination of the Mediterranean—an ambition which led to a fatal dissipation of imperial energies.

In violation of his oath, Henry the Lion had returned to Germany in 1190, and taken possession of the lands of count Adolf III of Holstein, who had accompanied Frederick on crusade. Although king Henry did obtain the support of a majority of the princes against Henry the Lion, it was clear that the latter could not be dealt with easily or quickly. As part of the treaty of Fulda (1190), according to which the city of Lübeck was divided between Henry the Lion and count Adolf, king Henry took the two sons of Henry the Lion as hostages. In the autumn of 1190, the king journeyed to Italy, obtained the imperial crown from Pope Celestinus III, failed to conquer Apulia, and returned to Germany in the following year. However, Henry, the oldest son of Henry the Lion, had preceded him. He had accompanied Henry VI to Italy, had fled while the emperor was sick with malaria at Naples, returned to Saxony, and spread the rumour of the emperor's death, thus stoking the turmoil which again prevailed in that duchy. The present intrigue against the emperor was of truly international scope, comprising, apart from the Welfs and their allies among the German princes, the Pope, Tancred of Sicily, and Richard I of England.

Good fortune, however, played into the hands of the emperor. When duke Leopold of Austria had his banner hoisted on a tower in Acre which his men had stormed, Richard had it torn down—motivated, perhaps, by enmity toward an opponent of Guido of Lusignan's pretensions to leadership of the crusading armies, perhaps by enmity toward an ally of king Philip of France or toward an enemy of Henry the Lion. At any rate, on his way to England in 1192 Richard was shipwrecked and had to make his way through the domains of Leopold. He was recognized, arrested near Vienna, imprisoned in the castle of Dürnstein on the Danube, then turned over to the emperor. At

The Chivalric Period

one blow the princes' plots against Henry were crippled. In 1194 Richard obtained his liberty in return for a ransom of 150,000 marks, and there followed a reconciliation between the emperor and the house of the Welfs.

The internal affairs of Germany settled, Henry planned a crusade. Before such a venture could be undertaken, however, the matter of succession had to be put on a firm footing, all the more so since the unity of Sicily and the empire depended on the re-establishment of imperial succession by heredity. Should the princes elect another dynasty to the imperial throne, this union would be severed, since Henry's claim to Sicily was purely dynastic, binding Sicily to the Hohenstaufens. The princes as well as the Pope, however, could not be won for such a sweeping change in the very fundament of the monarchy; but by an eventual reduction of his demands, Henry did secure the election of his son Frederick as king in 1196. The crusade which Henry had planned did not materialize. In 1197 an uprising in Sicily demanded his presence, and on September 28 of that year he died in Messina.

Frederick was three years old at the time of Henry's death, and the empress Constance died the following year. The responsibility of a regency therefore rested with Henry's brother, Philip of Swabia. The support given him by the princes averted a state of total chaos for the moment. In fact, it was at the urging of the princes that he finally consented to be crowned in 1198. In the same year, however, Innocent III ascended the papal throne. Innocent was an adherent of the old Gregorian view of the empire and the functions of the emperor, and was, moreover, acutely aware of the dangers facing the papacy by an empire comprising Germany, central Italy, and Sicily. The Pope had an ally in Richard I of England, who backed Otto of Brunswick, duke of Aquitaine, earl of York, and count of Poitou, the second son of Henry the Lion, as anti-king. Otto subscribed completely to the political theories of Innocent III. Once again Germany

Medieval Civilization in Germany

was wracked by civil wars, this time fostered by England and the papacy on the one hand, and Philip Augustus of France, backing Philip of Swabia, on the other.

Upon the death of Richard in 1199, Otto's cause was as good as lost. Neither the Pope's recognition of Otto in 1201, nor his excommunication of Philip and his followers had much effect. In 1204 some of Otto's most powerful supporters, including his brother, the count palatine Henry, the archbishop of Cologne, and the king of Bohemia changed allegiance. By 1207 the Pope was negotiating with Philip, from whom he now lifted the excommunication. However, on June 21, 1208, Philip, aged 31, was assassinated. The murderer was the count palatine Otto of Wittelsbach, the cause a personal one.

In the choice between total chaos and Otto of Brunswick, the latter seemed the lesser of two evils. He was elected in the same year, and received the imperial crown in 1209 in return for his

Fig. 34 Signature of Philip of Swabia on a deed from Aachen dated January 12, 1204. Legend: 'Signum domini Philippi secundi romanorum regis invictissimi' (the Roman emperor Philippus, 244–249, counted as first) (after Jäger)

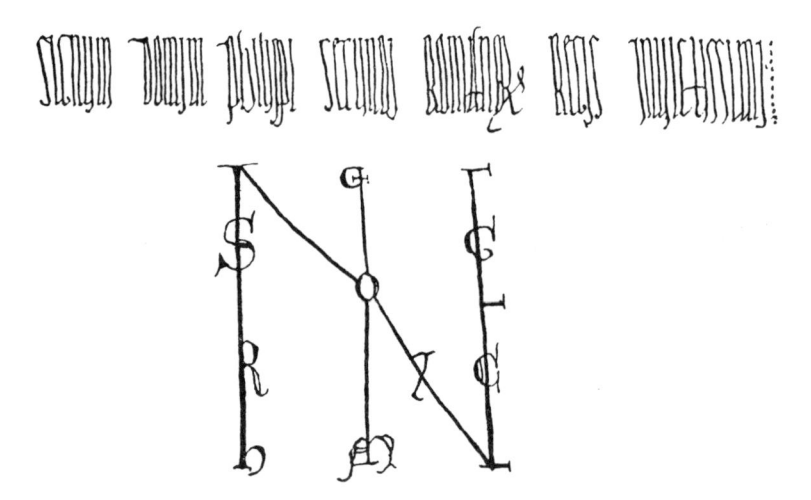

recognition of the expansion of the papal state over Umbria, Spoleto and Ancona to the Adriatic, his guarantee of 'free' episcopal elections, his acknowledgment of the independence of the ecclesiastical judicial system, and other concessions. The attitude of Otto IV toward the papacy now changed completely, just as his own role had changed from head of a party to emperor. He possessed himself of the still disputed parts of the Mathildine inheritance, subjected Apulia and Calabria to his rule, and in 1210 was in a position to consider a Sicilian campaign, in order to displace the Hohenstaufens there. At this point he was, of course, promptly excommunicated. French financial support, as well as that of the archbishop of Mainz, king Ottokar of Bohemia, the dukes of Bavaria and Austria, among others, resuscitated the Hohenstaufen cause in Germany.

The son of Henry VI, Frederick, was now eighteen years old. In 1211, in Nuremberg, he was elected king and *in imperatorem coronandum*, re-elected *rex Romanorum* in Frankfurt in 1212 and crowned at Mainz. During the few months which he had spent on German soil preceding his coronation, his supporters had increased rapidly from the sixty horsemen with whom he had arrived at Constance. Otto's cause, supported by king John of England, who had landed in Poitou in 1214, however, received its death-blow from France. In the same year, at the battle of Bouvines, Philip Augustus decisively defeated the German army and transmitted the damaged imperial golden eagle, which had been left on the field of battle, to Frederick—a symbolic act which was not lost on contemporaries.

Frederick, remarkably learned and polished in manner and expression, author of the famous *De arte venandi cum avibus*, a manual of falconry, was reared in Sicily and regarded that island and Italy as his homeland. Imperial policy accordingly revolved around Sicilian and Italian issues, while Germany and its affairs assumed a secondary role. German *ministeriales* in the administration of Italy were replaced by Sicilian officials, in German internal affairs the princes were allowed to benefit from the neglect of monarchical interests, and Frederick even refused the advantages derivable from an alliance with the rapidly growing and prospering cities against the princes. He had need of the support of the princes for his Italian and Sicilian undertakings, and he was willing to buy this support with concessions in Germany which he would have deemed unthinkable in Sicily.

One result of these policies was the disappearance of whatever unified character the empire may have exhibited in previous reigns. From 1220 to 1232 Frederick concerned himself primarily with Sicilian and Italian affairs, while his son Henry took over the rule of Germany. The monarchy was even divested of its support from the German Church. The Golden Bull of Eger (1213) in which Frederick made the same concessions to the Pope as Otto IV did in 1209, and the *Confoederatio cum principibus ecclesiasticis* (1220) removed the control of the king over elections and territories of the bishops, who ceased to represent royalist views and allied themselves with the princes. In the *Statutum in favorem principum* (1232) the renunciation, on the part of the king, of such rights as the levying of taxes and the building of castles on episcopal domains was extended to apply to the domains of all princes. Henry, intending to stem the rising tide of princely power, not only incurred the enmity of such magnates as the duke of Bavaria, but also was countered by his father, who could ill afford the loss of the princes' support. Henry finally revolted, surrendered in 1235, was imprisoned, and died in Apulia in 1242.

At this time the princes were concerned mainly with the consolidation of their position, in which they were aided in 1239 by the excommunication of Frederick, and the papal nomination, in 1246, of the landgrave of Thuringia, Heinrich Raspe, as anti-king. As for the rest, Frederick left the affairs of Germany to his son Conrad, who, after the death of Heinrich Raspe in 1247, continued the war against the next anti-king, count William of

Plate 50

Holland. While war raged in Germany and the princes displayed an agility in changing sides prompted solely by the chances of territorial gain, Frederick died in December 1250 near Luceria. He was succeeded by his son Conrad IV, who left Germany in the following year to spend most of the remaining four years of his life in putting down a revolt in Sicily. The papacy now had little difficulty in achieving its aim of eradicating that 'nest of vipers', the Hohenstaufen dynasty, from the face of the earth.

Meanwhile a major shift in population was in progress. German expansion into Slav territory had continued without great interruptions since its beginnings in the Ottonian period. The complexion of this eastward movement, however, changed considerably in the course of time. The existence of surplus goods, the need for markets, and the attractions of frontier freeholds for the small peasant were incentives which increasingly replaced the desire for simple conquest to exact tribute from the vanquished. In short, conquest was succeeded as a goal by colonization. Nevertheless, not all later phases of the expansion were characterized by peaceful settlement. The princes of the Church, particularly the bishops of Magdeburg, Brandenburg and Halberstadt, called for a crusade, which took place in 1147, against the *crudelissimi gentiles* and their heathen misdeeds.

Christianization of the Slavs was the principal goal of the order of Teutonic Knights. Independent from both papacy and empire, the order rapidly subjugated Prussia, Livland, Kurland, and Estonia. The fact that these possessions soon yielded a surplus of agricultural products forced the order into international commerce and even occasional competition with the Hanseatic League. Gradually, the order's original purpose faded under political and economic pressure, and Christianization of the native populace became the aim of Slav princes, such as king Jagello of Poland.

The speed and effectiveness of the colonization of Slav territory is attested by the fact that, even against the opposition of Polish

Fig. 35 Saxon colonizer with Wendish prisoner. The Saxon is characterized by means of the large knife (sahs), the Wend is depicted with a white cloak and leg-ties, which were regarded as heathen and prohibited to the Teutonic Knights. From the Heidelberg Sachsenspiegel *(after Jäger)*

clerics and nobility, 255 villages and 77 cities governed according to German laws had sprung into being by the middle of the fourteenth century. At the same time, it is estimated that Poland and Galicia together contained more than 1,500 newly founded villages under German law. In the territory of the Teutonic Knights, the number of such villages is estimated at over 1,000, with 93 towns. It is probable that approximately two million peasants left Germany to settle permanently on Slav soil.

Frederick Barbarossa's denial of the claims of Hadrian IV had been based on secular arguments. For the first time an emperor had countered a Pope not as *rex et sacerdos,* implying that his status was no different from the Pope's, but as *rex,* relying on the sufficient applicability of non-theocratic legal argument. A new secularism, a readiness to view the world and temporal existence as more than a pale shadow of a more important existence beyond it, gradually began to manifest itself in all forms of human expression, whether political, philosophical, or artistic. Emanating from France, it spread into Germany and much of the rest of Europe, together with the ideals and fashions of chivalry.

The significance ascribed to temporal existence is reflected with particular clarity in the development of historiography. The annalistic style, the chronological listing of events without

Fig. 36 Peasants and plough, thirteenth century. Heidelberg Sachsenspiegel *(after Jäger)*

Fig. 37   Peasants building a village. The lord of the village grants the founder the hereditary right to taxation by a deed 'ego dei gratia' with triangular seals. From the Heidelberg Sachsenspiegel *(after Jäger)*

commentary, which still characterized the chronicle of Hermann of Reichenau in the eleventh century, was gradually replaced by interpretative, often propagandistic historical treatments. Commentary already plays a modest role in the *Gesta Hammaburgensis* of Adam of Bremen, which was written between 1075 and 1085. An exclusively political orientation is discernible in Lampert of Hersfeld's *Annales* (1077), in which he sought to win the reader for the cause of Rudolf of Rheinfelden against Henry IV. Frankly propagandistic is Bruno's *Bellum Saxonicum*, in which the Saxon author made no secret of his hatred for Henry IV and his Swabian *ministeriales*. The greatest medieval German chronicles—the *Chronica* of Otto of Freising and the *Gesta Friderici* of the same author, continued by Rahewîn—are a particularly good example of the change in attitude toward temporal existence. Otto, bishop of Freising, was a grandson of Henry IV, half-brother of Conrad III, and uncle of Frederick Barbarossa. His first work, composed between 1143 and 1146, stands entirely in the tradition of the Augustinian concept of history: the doomed *civitas terrena* confronted by the eternal *civitas Dei*. Ten years later, however, bishop Otto presents the first years of Barbarossa's reign in a totally secular, optimistic light. The great popularity of such works as the Low German *Sachsenspiegel*, a legal compendium composed by Eike of Repgow *c.* 1225, which inspired such similar compendia as the *Deutschenspiegel* and *Schwabenspiegel,* testifies no less to the increased weight given to secular affairs.

The socio-political organization of Germany now reached the degree of feudal integration which France had reached more than a hundred years before. Early in the century, the nominalism of Roscellinus and Peter Abelard expressed a positive evaluation of evidence provided through the senses: Abelard characterized the position of the realist William of Champeaux as 'contradicting nature in every respect'.[3] Later, under the impact of the newly translated works of Aristotle, the university of Paris became the principal battleground on which Philosophy emancipated itself from Theology, and the seven liberal arts, formerly the handmaidens of Theology, were placed in a position of independence. The increase in the secular orientation of man's thinking is no less expressed in the sudden rise of Mariolatry. Christ, the Judge, was felt to be too far removed from man and his world, while Mary, who bore the sorrows of a mother, appeared more human, more approachable as an individual. Gothic architecture, likewise, had its beginnings in the Île de France, in Abbot Suger's Saint-Denis.

Fig. 38

The individual, that which can be perceived through the senses, became the determinant of artistic endeavour in general. Of course, not all forms of expression with this tendency spread from France over Germany with the same speed. Gothic art and architecture were perhaps the slowest to develop a distinctive style. Not until the fourteenth century did German Gothic forms begin to evolve from the basic French concept. However, Gothic architecture closely conforming to French models, made its

Fig. 38 The spread of Gothic architecture on the European continent from the thirteenth to the sixteenth century. The territory of the Empire in the fourteenth century

appearance promptly in Germany. Not only were the forms alike, but also the socio-economic basis for Gothic architecture was the same in Germany as in France. Whereas Romanesque architecture was primarily monastic, Gothic was predominantly urban. While Romanesque found its most eloquent expression in abbey churches, Gothic sought its formulation in the cathedral. The city was rapidly coming of age, and the pursuits of the bourgeoisie, as well as the realistic view of the world which these pursuits demanded, added not a little to the generally increasing awareness of this world as a value in itself.

The technical innovations, without which Gothic architecture —entirely new in its treatment of space and surface—is unthinkable, are the pointed arch and, above all, the rib-vault. Groin-vaulting, like rib-vaulting, directs the thrust of weight upon it to its four angles, but it is lighter, easier to construct, and it reinforces the vault precisely where it is weakest: at the groins and the summit. Moreover, it can cover any space and provides added resistance to the effects of frost, subsidence, or deformation. The walls now cease to function merely as supports, static space-dividers and surfaces for decoration, and become dynamic. No longer simply surfaces, their components—arches, windows, columns, and not least the demi-colonnes from which the ribs of the vaults spring—endow the whole with an upward movement. At the same time, interior space is decompartmentalized: the new wall treatment, emphasizing dynamic components rather than static planes, as well as the homogeneity of these components throughout the cathedral, impart a high degree of transparency to each part of the structure. The buttresses made necessary by the thrusts exerted upon the walls, as well as the many breaks in the wall surface, the windows, galleries, etc., cause the exterior to appear transparent: the shell of the structure, consisting, as it were, of an outer network of buttresses and *arcs-boutants,* and a highly textured inner layer, is in appearance diaphanous. In contrast, the Romanesque structure, even late Romanesque, is defined internally and externally by comparatively unbroken walls: windows are small and placed at greater intervals, buttresses massive and part of the walls, so that the interior presents a compartmentalized, static appearance, and the exterior of the structure defies the surrounding world with the aloofness of an impenetrable object.

The highly textured walls of the Gothic cathedral precluded mural painting. Its place was taken by stained glass windows, which, though they admitted more light than Romanesque windows, suffused the interior with soft and colourful illumination rather than bathing it in brilliance. These windows, apart from serving as decorative and didactic substitutes for wall painting, served a tectonic function by contributing to the diaphanous effect of the walls. By virtue of their size, number, and structural integration in the textured walls, the windows no longer appeared as openings, as breaks in solid substance, but as part of the wall texture. The wall, therefore, in its lightness, appears to let light filter through. The wall of the Gothic cathedral reveals in its function a total reversal of the relationship between the tectonic and the decorative. In Romanesque churches the wall functions as bearer of paintings, which obscure or change its tectonic structure. The Gothic wall is the decoration itself; the decorative resides in the tectonic.

The symbolism of Romanesque murals, moreover, is embodied in the Gothic structure itself. The concept of the church as symbol—'ecclesia materialis significat ecclesiam spiritualem'— is not limited to the period of Gothic architecture, but applies equally to preceding periods. The manner in which this symbolism was expressed in the Gothic church, however, was new. Whereas the symbolism of Romanesque churches is pictorial rather than tectonic, that of Gothic structures lies in the basic form of the structure itself, as well as in the role played by light. The Gothic architect determined all proportions of his structure on the basis of one fundamental form, such as certain polygons and, particularly, the square.[4] The proportionate relationship of each part of the structure to each other part, determined on the basis of one figure, symbolically reflected the order of creation, the harmony of the universe. The symbolic prerequisite of order and value, however, was light. Both Hugh of St Victor and Thomas Aquinas regarded proportion and light, i.e. clarity, as the principal attributes of beauty. 'Light, which is the first visible,' says the philosopher Witelo (c. 1230–1275) in his *Perspectiva*, 'determines beauty. Sun, moon, and stars appear to us to be beautiful only because of their light. Colour contributes to beauty. Green, red, and the other brilliant colours present to the eye the form of light which is appropriate to them.' Unlike the light-symbolism of Romanesque art, which sought to give form to the contrast between light and darkness, Gothic light-symbolism was based on the concept of light as all-pervasive, and Gothic architecture made use of light alone as a structural element. The Gothic structure, itself a tectonic symbol of order, suffused by light, is a symbolic model of creation.

The architects of the earliest Gothic cathedrals in Germany were restricted in their application of the principles of Gothic which they had learned in France, since many of the great German churches were already in the process of being built around the turn of the century. The cathedral of Magdeburg was the only major church which could be built from the ground up according to the new principles. Those of Mainz, Worms, Strassburg, Bamberg, and Naumburg offered the architect opportunity for varying degrees of adaptation of the Gothic style to the structure which already existed in part.

Of particular influence in Germany were the Cistercian builders, who were principally responsible for the construction of the cathedrals of Magdeburg and Bamberg. The conservatism of Cistercian architecture, with its avoidance of complex buttressing to counter the thrust of the vault's weight, and its adherence to Romanesque use of the relatively unbroken wall as support, determined the adaptation of the Gothic style to the existing Romanesque structures. A rapid development of Gothic in Germany was impeded not only by the need for its adaptation, but also by the continuance of Romanesque in public favour: the purely Romanesque east choir of the cathedral of Bamberg and the west choir at Mainz are contemporary with the first Gothic structures in Germany.

The Gothic style was not conclusively pre-eminent until the construction of the cathedral of Cologne, which was begun in 1248. The architect who planned this building, one Master

Plate 53

Gerhard, chose the cathedral of Amiens as his model though he was determined to improve upon it. But the plans for four aisles and twin towers were too ambitious to be systematically carried out. Once the choir and façade for the two towers were built, the structure remained a torso, to be completed between 1842 and 1880. Nevertheless, Gerhard's intention of surpassing Amiens is clearly demonstrated in the stress on verticality: the demi-colonnes rise to the base of the cross-ribs without interruption. Similarly, the preponderance of the towers over the rest of the structure, which was to become a characteristic of German cathedral architecture in the next two centuries, is not to be found in any French cathedral.

In 1275 the nave of the cathedral of Strassburg was completed. In contrast to the emphasis on verticality in Cologne cathedral, the stress at Strassburg was on breadth. Despite the uninterrupted course of the demi-colonnes to the *impostes d'arc*, the desired impression of breadth is achieved through the dominance of the triforia. The importance of the towers for the entire structure, however, is almost as great as in the case of Cologne. To be sure, the upper part of the tower-façade is a product of the fourteenth century and deviates from the original plans. But the intention of the planning architect reveals itself in the emphasis given to the three deep portals with their statues, as well as in the stress on verticality provided by the delicate shafts which, like the strings of a harp, form a close array in front of the walls and thereby contribute to their diaphanous appearance. The statuary here, even such personifications as Ecclesia and Synagoga, reflect the concern of the sculptor with the realities of form: the human body, the fall of drapery, and the subtle revelation of the body beneath it.

Plates 56, 57

The sculpture in the tympanum of the south portal of Strassburg cathedral demonstrates the union of Romanesque principles of structure with Gothic 'realism'. The twelve Apostles surround one side of the death-bed of Mary. In their midst is

Plate 55

Christ, at each end of the bed an Apostle bends over Mary, and in front sits Mary Magdelene, wringing her hands in sorrow. The symmetric design fits the semicircle of the tympanum. At the same time, however, the expressions on the faces of the Apostles realistically portray sorrow, and the folds of their garments betray a concern, on the part of the artist, with the bodies beneath them as well as with the realistic representation of the drapery.

The 'acceptance and reconciliation of contradictory possibilities' (Panofsky), Romanesque design with Gothic representation, or—in the case of Cologne cathedral—the solution of a technical problem of proportion by a combination of the cylindrical *pilier cantonné* of Amiens and its four shafts with the continuous shafts of St Denis, reflects a scholastic method of reconciliation of conflicting authorities: the so-called *Sic-et-Non* method.[5]

The reconciliation of contradictory arguments could only be carried out within a schematic framework of argumentation such as the structure which characterizes the great *Summae* of this period—'an arrangement according to a system of homologous parts and parts of parts' (Panofsky). Each part and part of a part stands in a given relationship to the whole, just as each part of a Gothic cathedral is proportionately related to each other part and to the entire structure.

The necessity for syntheses, for reconciliation between tradition or authority on the one hand and new knowledge or new attitudes on the other, also made itself felt in scholastic philosophy. The impact of the works of Aristotle, which began to be translated from the Arabic in the first half of the twelfth century and, freed from Neo-platonic accretions, continued to be translated directly from the Greek in the thirteenth, brought about a rift in philosophical thought. In the first place, the works of Aristotle strengthened the arts curriculum to such a degree that philosophy, embodying the physical sciences as well as the arts enriched by Aristotle, could be severed from theology, regarded as independent and offering explanations at variance with those of theology.

The Chivalric Period

This was the position of 'Latin Averroism'. Secondly, all that conflicted with the teachings of St Augustine could be expunged from those of Aristotle, and the latter could be accepted, along with the former, subject to the primary stricture that only through grace can temporal knowledge and the temporal existence which alone it elucidates, be transcended. This was the Augustinian standpoint. A third manner of coming to terms with Aristotle was to attempt an integration of his metaphysics with Christianity, which was accomplished by the Thomists.

The achievement of the Franciscan St Bonaventure in adapting Aristotle to Augustinianism was paralleled by that of the Christianization of Aristotle at the hands of the Dominicans Albertus Magnus and his pupil Thomas Aquinas. The difficulty which the works of Aristotle posed for theological learning is demonstrated by the ban against the study of Aristotle in the Dominican order—an order founded for the purpose of furthering theological study—in 1228. But the attitudes of the members of the Dominican order toward Aristotle were as inconsistent as those of the Franciscans. It was Albert's purpose to present and clarify the works of Aristotle for the brothers of his order. His primary concern, therefore, was to supply commentaries rather than to contribute to philosophical thought. Nevertheless, in his stress on experimentation, in his distinction between science and revelation, he goes considerably further than his predecessors.

Albert was born in Lauingen, Swabia, in 1206, studied philosophy at Padua and entered the Dominican order in 1223. He taught at Cologne, then at the University of Paris (1240–1248), where he was the teacher of Thomas Aquinas. He returned to the Dominican School at Cologne and taught there until his consecration as bishop of Regensburg in 1260. Two years later he resigned in order to return to his position at Cologne, where he died in 1280.

Albert's most significant contribution was his acceptance of Moses Maimonides' distinction between the attributes of faith and reason, and the inviolate nature of each. Philosophy and theology were not to be regarded as in competition with one another, but each as competent in its own sphere: philosophy, i.e. reason, in natural experience, theology, i.e. faith, in revealed matters. He found it impossible to comment with certainty and on the basis of rationality on matters such as the creation of the world. In sacred doctrine, on the other hand, 'Albert does not resort to argumentation in order to cause this science to invent new truths by rational argumentation from principles; rather, he attributes to theology argumentation in a polemic sense, in view of refuting as erroneous the conclusions opposed to the principles of theology.'[6]

Albert's view of the nature of the soul clearly marks his unique position in the history of scholasticism as neither entirely Thomistic, nor entirely non-Augustinian: 'If we consider the soul in itself, we shall agree with Plato; if we consider it as a form giving life to the body, we shall agree with Aristotle' (*Sum. Theol.* II, 12, 69, 2, 12). The Neoplatonism implied here as well as, for instance, in the belief in the possibility of a graduated order of knowledge ascending to knowledge of God as the ultimate cause of the soul's knowledge, had its effect on a number of disciples. Among the most notable Albertists are Hugh Ripelin, also called Hugh of Strassburg, probably the author of a tremendously popular *Compendium theologiae*, his favourite student Ulrich Engelbrecht, or Ulrich of Strassburg, author of a *Summa, On the Supreme Good*, and Dietrich of Vrieberg. The last-named, particularly in his work *On the Intellect and the Intelligible,* was also heavily influenced by Proclus, and exemplifies, perhaps more than his contemporaries, the unabated vitality of Neoplatonism.

The most important of Albert's pupils was, of course, Thomas Aquinas, in whose thought one can note a tendency which parallels the realism of Gothic art, the concern with the individual, the unique, rather than with the generalized, the type. Thomas, instead of disregarding the senses and the world which could be known through them, and rejecting them as 'unreal', regarded them as yielding evidence of the 'real' in its functions. Instead of refusing to avail himself of the tools at hand and attempting to explain God on the basis of an assumed inexplicability, he turned to His creation, proceeding from the individual to the universal. In short, for Thomas the individual reflects the universal.

The concern with the phenomena of this world is also increasingly expressed in the literature of the period. This does not mean that the literature of the preceding century consisted mainly of religious matter and that this was suddenly replaced by the expression of predominantly wordly concerns. Mundane matters and the worldly pageant no doubt played a considerable role during the eleventh and early twelfth centuries, but they were seldom cast in written form. The art of writing was, in general, practised by monastic scribes, monks whose duty it was to copy manuscripts or who were called upon to compose a poem. Obviously, the manuscripts copied, the poems composed, and the works preserved by these monks were mainly works of religious nature or ecclesiastical interest. Heroic lays, epic poems recited orally, and lusty drinking songs no doubt existed in plenty, but these seldom found their way onto parchment. During the latter part of the twelfth century, however, the growth of trade, the steadily increasing complexity of political and judicial administration, and—during the thirteenth century—the rise of the universities, led to a demand for written documents which could no longer be met by monastic scribes.[7] The ability to write became more common, and secular *scriptoria* sprang up and thrived in the cities and around the schools and universities. Works of a worldly nature, as well as many which were critical of the Church, or expressed attitudes of which the Church disapproved, now readily found their way onto paper or parchment.

Fig. 39

Among the epics, which were no doubt orally recited for generations before they were written down during the latter half of the twelfth century, were the so-called *Spielmannsepen* or

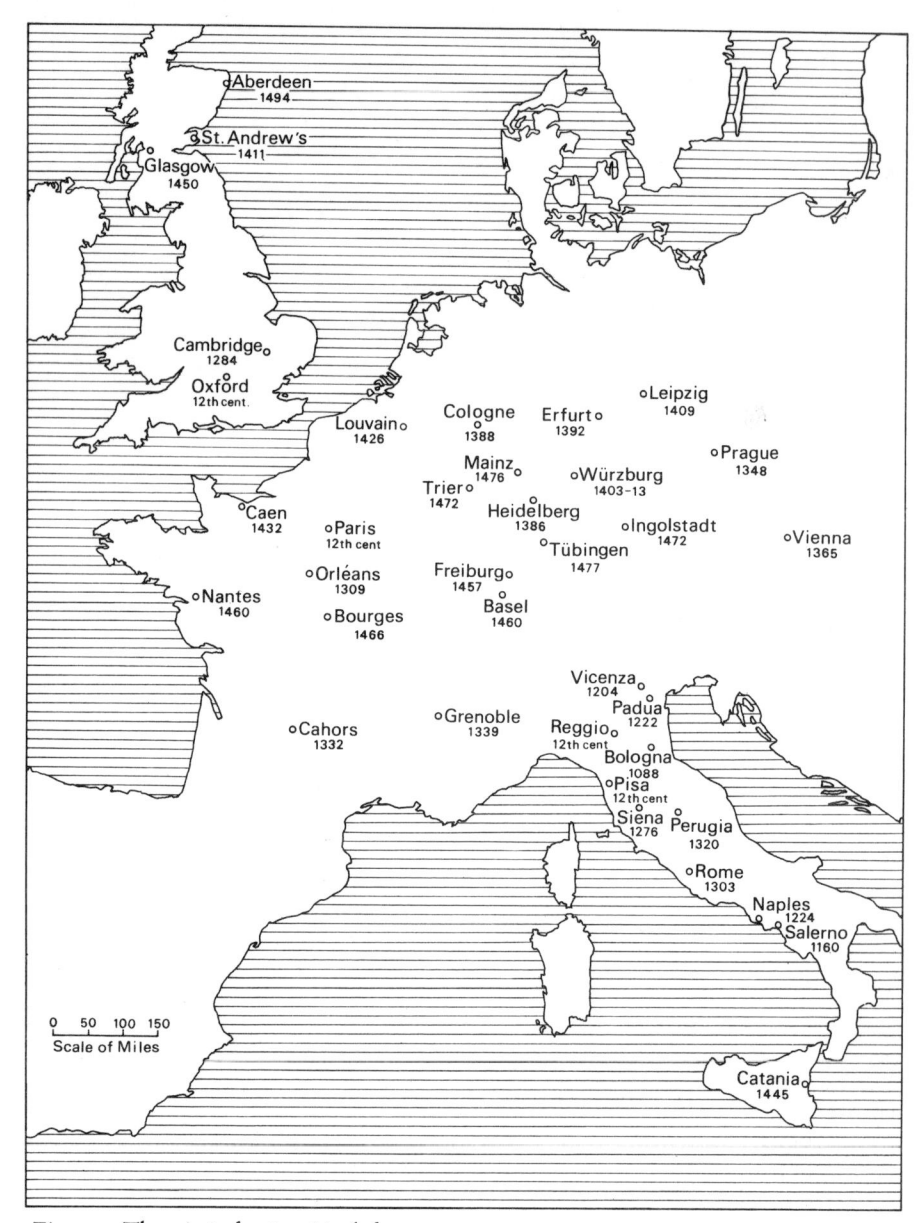

Fig. 39   The principal universities before 1500

Fig. 40 Children's game. From Herrad of Landsberg, Hortus deliciarum *(after Schultz)*

'gleemen's epics'. Literary historians of the nineteenth century ascribed these relatively short epics to the *Spielleute* or gleemen. There were indeed great numbers of these *joculatores, jongleurs,* or minstrels roaming the country, telling tales, performing tricks, and selling baubles, but it now appears unlikely that the authors of these so-called *Spielmannsepen* are to be sought among that motley crew. At best, these illiterate, vagrant entertainers can be regarded as reciters, disseminators of these epics. Epic poems, of course, can be orally created, transmitted and, in transmission, recreated by illiterate reciters.[8] This was probably the case with the original narrative stratum of some of these epics, a stratum which contains, in addition to the familiar motif of bride-abduction, a high density of oral formulae and other stylistic characteristics which indicate oral transmission. But superimposed upon this orally transmitted narrative stratum is—in some cases—an adaptation which has its origin in writing.

The best of these epics, *König Rother,* is a relatively simple composition of about 1160, probably by a Rhenish poet. It relates the story of king Rother's expedition to win a bride and the ruses and abductions he resorted to. Of the three other poems usually subsumed with *König Rother* under the heading *Spielmannsepen,*

Fig. 41 Miniature from the Heidelberg manuscript of the Rolandslied *(after Schultz)*

the tale of *Salman and Morolf*—Solomon and his cunning brother Morolf—treats a similar theme: Solomon's repeated loss of his faithless wife and her recapture by Morolf. The other two poems of the group, *St Oswald* and *Orendel*, are examples of a literate poet's adaptation of orally transmitted material to his own purposes. In both cases, the oral stratum is represented by a tale of winning a bride, but a clerical 'message' has been superimposed: in the case of *St Oswald*, the trappings of a saint's legend, in that of *Orendel*, clerical propaganda for the relic of the seamless cloak of Christ at Trier. A fascination with the riches and marvels of the Near East is common to all these works, and testifies to the effect of the tales of returning crusaders. The time of composition of these epics in the form in which they are trans-

Fig. 42 Another miniature from the Heidelberg manuscript of the Rolandslied *(after Schultz)*

Fig. 43 Right: bestowal of the accolade, British Museum, Cotton. Nero.D.I. (after Schultz)

The Chivalric Period

mitted is uncertain. They survive only in manuscripts and prints of the fifteenth and sixteenth centuries, but are usually assumed to have originated in the latter part of the twelfth century.

The interests and passions aroused by the early crusades were expressed by a translation of the classic epic of crusading, the *Chanson de Roland*. Probably about 1170 the priest Konrad of Regensburg wrote his *Rolandslied* in the archaic style favoured at the court of Henry the Lion. The spirit of French national pride that pervades the original, and which could hold neither appeal nor interest for German readers, yielded, under Konrad's pen, to increased emphasis on Christian militancy, and on the mission of the crusaders in combatting evil as personified by the Saracens, a combat in which death is martyrdom.

Figs. 41, 42

Ten years before the *Rolandslied* was written, the first literary symptoms of a thoroughly secularized society appeared in Austria. The increase in the number and power of the *ministeriales*, and developments in warfare which made armour and extensive training necessary, led to the formation of a social class in which membership was determined not by the holding of land or even by birth, but by training. This class, the knights, united in their class-consciousness by the ostensibly common cause of the crusades, was the principal social and artistic determinant throughout the latter part of the twelfth and the first half of the

Fig. 44 Hohenstaufen knight, from the Annals of Genoa, *Bibl. Nat., Paris (after Schultz)*

Fig. 43

thirteenth century. No one was born a knight, knighthood had to be achieved, at least formally, even though one was a prince. Since the criterion of worthiness was—in theory at least—achievement, certain ideals of achievement developed, which served as the mark of a knight. These ideals, consisting in large part of behavioural forms, were expressed and analyzed in the form as well as the content of works of art.

The most typical positive expression of one of these behavioural forms—that of courtly love—was the courtly lyric. Nourished by motifs and themes current in the Arabic lyric of Moorish Spain and in Ovid, this genre of highly complex and sophisticated lyric poetry developed rapidly in Provence. From southern France

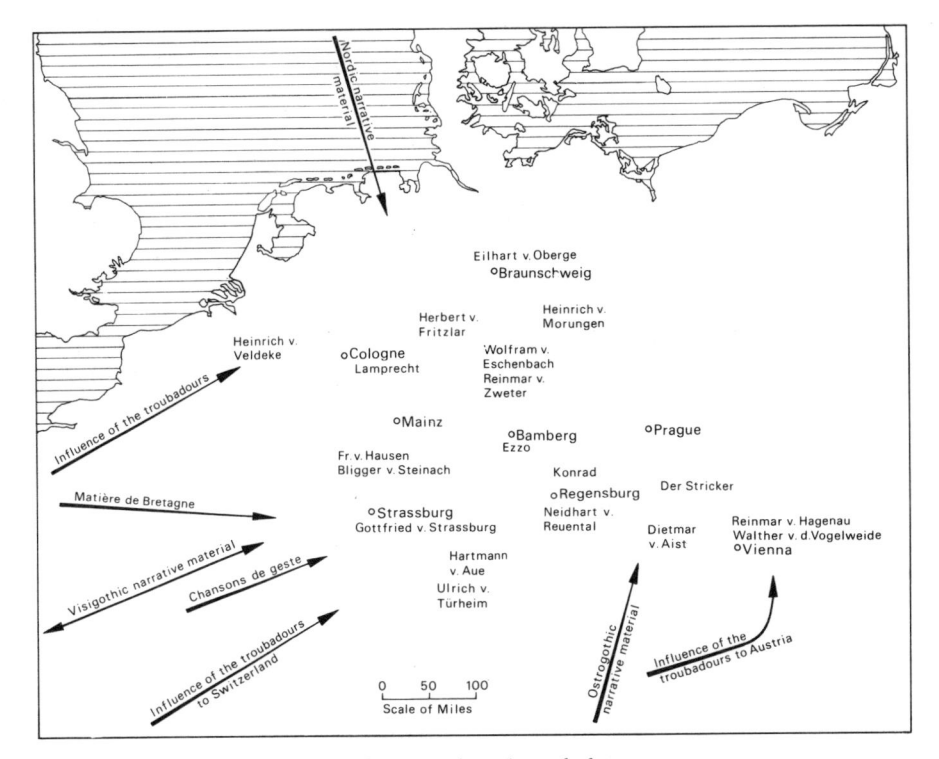

Fig. 45   Principal representatives of pre-courtly and courtly literature

it spread northwards and into the Netherlands, and eastwards, along the trade routes across northern Italy into Austria.

The courtly love lyric must, however, be distinguished from the lyric in general. The differences between this sub-genre and other types of lyric poetry are thematic, formal and developmental, besides being functional. Thus the lusty, personal poems of the greatest medieval German lyric poet who wrote in Latin, the so-called Archipoeta, as well as most of the Latin poetry of the *vagantes* transmitted in the famous manuscript of the *Carmina Burana*, have little to do with courtly poetry beyond the use of some common funds of motifs and rhetorical devices. The lyrics of the pre-eminent poet of the Netherlands, Heinrich of Veldeke, likewise seem to have exerted very little influence on the development of the German courtly lyric. The principal influence emanated from Austria, where the early courtly love lyric—early *Minnesang*—flourished.

Literary historians customarily view the products of this early stage in the development of Middle High German *Minnesang* as hybrid manifestations of a native lyric tradition and elements of the Provençal lyric of the troubadours. Since no 'native', i.e. pre-courtly, lyric is transmitted in the vernacular, that which is 'native' is adduced from the early examples of the courtly lyric and is then used to characterize the poems from which it was adduced. We need only glance at the works themselves, unblurred by such pre-conceptions, to recognize the presence of all the principal elements of courtly love and its poetry in these early lyrics.

One of the most famous and earliest poems of *Minnesang* is the so-called 'Falcon Song' of the Kürenberger, an Austrian who seems to have lived around 1160:

> I raised me a falcon   for more than a year.
> When I had tamed him   as I would have him be
> and I had dressed his feathers   with richly golden bands,
> aloft he soared, on high,   and flew to other lands.
>
> Since then I saw the falcon   gracefully flying:
> he sported upon his foot   silken tyings
> and his coat of feathers   glittered golden.
> May God bring together   who ever lovers would remain.

It is possible, at first glance, to read these eight lines in several different ways. Some critics, for instance, have proposed a reading of the poem as a so-called *Wechsel*, a subgenre of the courtly love lyric, in which the speakers, often linked by a messenger, address each other in the third person. This reading posits two speakers, a lady and her lover, among whom the two stanzas are apportioned. The falcon serves as messenger, sent out by the lady and perceived by her lover. Several elements contradict this interpretation: the sense of the text does not demand an interpretation of the falcon as messenger, nor is it necessary to assume two speakers. The most salient objection to this interpretation, however, rests on the meaning of the words 'flew to other lands' (MHG 'vlouc in andriu lant'). This formulation is a technical expression in falconry and signifies a flight of the falcon against the will of its master. If the falcon functioned as messenger in this poem, he could scarcely be said to have flown away against his mistress' will. The same objection invalidates the reading of the text as spoken by the lady, who sends out her falcon and sees him returning later, adorned by her lover. The principal support for this interpretation lies in the Middle High German description of his adornments in the second stanza as 'alrôt guldîn,' i.e. 'gilt throughout', which is understood to augment the 'guldine riemen', the 'golden bands' of the first stanza. The most common reading, however, assumes one speaker, the lady. The falcon serves as symbol for her lover, whom she has lost and whom she sees in the second stanza adorned by another, i.e. serving another mistress. From this viewpoint, however, it is difficult to explain the last line. The meaning paraphrased as 'may the best man, or rather woman, win' is scarcely credible in the context of a woman's mourning the loss of her lover to another.[9]

In any analysis of a medieval work of art, whether it be a painting or a poem, it is well to keep in mind the symbolic nature of medieval art. It is as great a mistake to inject notions of characterization in the modern sense into a reading of a medieval text as it is impossible to approach a medieval painting with notions of perspective. Three-dimensionality has as little to do with medieval poetry as with medieval painting. An 'interpretation' of the Falcon Song as a miniature chapter in a love affair, based either on the yearning of two lovers for one another, or on the melancholy, if not jealousy, of a woman, is a fabrication of the modern reader. It is natural to translate medieval symbolism automatically into modern three-dimensional symbolism, or to perceive the text in three-dimensional terms. The danger lies in the unawareness with which the poem is recast in terms of this perception. A valid analysis of any work of art calls for its full comprehension, and this can be achieved only if the interpreter is aware of the distinction between modern modes of perception and those of the cultural environment in which it originated.

The speaker in the Falcon Song is as little a 'character', i.e. an actual woman with feelings and hopes, as the depictions of human figures in a twelfth-century painting are intended to be portraits of individuals. To be sure, the speaker, the 'lyric I', is to be thought of as a woman. Beyond this, however, the function of this 'lyric I' is simply that of a figure—totally conceptualized, just as the figures in paintings of the period are vehicles for concepts, rather than embodiments of individual human experiences taking the form of individuals. The 'falcon' is not conclusively converted into a symbol until the last line. If this line is regarded as an organic part of the whole—which is not the case in most analyses of this poem—it clearly refers to the flight of the falcon by expressing the wish that what the flight symbolizes be remedied. Since this remedy is the union of two lovers, the falcon, who brought about the situation from which this wish arises, symbolizes a lover. The falcon as symbol for a lover is a common motif in medieval literature. Since, with very few exceptions, he symbolizes the male, the knight, it is legitimate to conceive of the speaker as the 'lady'. At this point it is essential to recall that falconry, which provides the symbolic structure for the whole poem, was not only an aristocratic sport, but was also considered as ennobling to its practitioner, since it demanded an extraordinary degree of self-discipline. Emperor Frederick II, in his book on falconry, *De arte venandi cum avibus,* clearly regarded the sport as an art which moulds character. He saw to it that young nobles who were to assume the highest governmental positions went through the rigorous training in self-discipline which falconry demanded.

Once the falcon has left the hand of its master, it is free. Only its own will can impel it to return, and it will only return to a master who controls himself, curbing any emotion which might frighten it. The wish of the last line is an organic part of the falconry symbolism in its assertion of the falcon's freedom: the union of two lovers, the falcon's return, is dependent not on compulsion emanating from one lover, not on duty of one towards the other, but on the will of the lover to return. Whether this in turn results in an act fulfilling the wish expressed by the supplicant depends, of course, on God.

In short, the poem gives symbolic structure to the concept of courtly love. Like falconry, courtly love (MHG *minne*) is a relationship into which the partners enter freely and which requires of them the constant exercise of self-discipline. This is not to say that sexuality played no role in courtly love; it was, in fact, of crucial importance, since the ultimate consummation of the relationship was sexual. But the sexual 'reward' had to be earned according to the rules governing the behaviour of both partners. The relationship of lady and lover is parallel to that of lord and vassal in feudal law. The lady plays the role of the lord, her lover that of the vassal. As in feudal law, each has rights as well as duties toward the other. The relationship itself, however, is entered into freely. Its continuance depends on the voluntary exercise of each partner's role in relation to the other within the rules as they were first extensively codified between 1174 and 1186 by Andreas Capellanus in his *De amore*, written for Marie de Champagne. Courtly love had nothing to do with marriage. The one is freely entered into and maintained, the other is not. The difference explains some of the rules of behaviour demanded of the lovers, such as the absolute secrecy of their identities.

In the Kürenberger's poem, the flight of the falcon creates a situation that has been deliberately brought about by the falconer, who is perfectly aware that the release of the bird may result in his flight 'to other lands'. Yet he does release him, in the knowledge that all depends upon the falcon's voluntary return. The speaker is conscious of the nature of her relationship to the falcon, i.e. the lover. In keeping with the didactic convention of courtly love, he has been ennobled by his relationship to her—the golden bands on his feathers constitute the corresponding symbol—and now he is free, beyond all compulsion. The expression of a wish —in the last line—is as far as she can go toward bringing about the desired result.

This interpretation is borne out by the construction of the poem. The very first line of all refers to a past situation. The second and third lines of both stanzas refer to the beauty of the falcon. The last line of the first and the first line of the second stanza depict the falcon in flight. Both lines, in the centre of the poem, are surrounded by the description of the falcon's beauty. The last line expresses the wish, in general terms, for a re-establishment of the past situation described in the first line, in the sense that this situation presupposes the presence of the falcon. It is also, however, the optative response to the last line of the first stanza, just as, in construction and its naming of the falcon-symbol, the first line of the second stanza corresponds to the first line of the first stanza. In short, the structure of the poem, is twofold: it is symmetrical as a whole as well as in its two parts, and it depicts a gesture—release, observation, and hope for the return of a falcon —symbolic of the essence of courtly love.

In the course of the last decades of the twelfth century, *Minnesang* became mannered under the influence of the Provençal lyric. This development reached its height in the poems of Reinmar of Hagenau (d. *c.* 1210) at the court of Vienna. The lyric now served the purpose, in part, of solving intellectual problems arising from the convention of courtly love. In one of Reinmar's poems, for instance, the conflict between the wish of the lover for the final 'reward' and his wish that his beloved remain a paragon of purity

The Chivalric Period

is elucidated, but there is no attempt to resolve the problem (Reinmar 165, 10–166, 6).

A pupil of Reinmar, Walther von der Vogelweide (d. *c.* 1230), altered this trend in the development of the lyric. He created a new type of poetic diction, in which the formal concepts of courtly love were expressed in a language that was stripped of its traditional formality. By this means he achieved a unique degree of immediacy by making possible an identification of poetic images with items of common experience. The figures in his poems are no longer the formal abstractions 'lady' and 'knight', but assume individual, human shape as girls and lovers. Moreover, the figures as well as their actions are part of the poetic environment, which is itself active. A linden tree and a meadow no longer merely symbolize spring or nature, as for instance in the poetry of Dietmar of Aist. They become active participants in the evocation of the experience; for instance, the grass and flowers, crushed and matted, testify to the meeting of lovers beneath the linden tree.

This type of depiction of an undisguised erotic situation has led some literary historians to see the beginning of so-called '*niedere Minne*', i.e. low courtly love, in the poetry of Walther. This is an error of some consequence. It is in part the advent of low courtly love, as in the lyrics of Neidhart of Reuenthal (d. *c.* 1250), which signals the decay of the classical courtly love lyric. Not only is Walther himself very outspoken against this type of poetry, but it is a mistake to equate eroticism or the introduction of figures not of a courtly social milieu with low courtly love. Walther, in integrating his figures in a natural environment, does lift them out of the traditional static, symbolic existence on the abstract, 'courtly' level. In fact, he expressly converts the concept of 'nobility' from its external, social connotation into a term expressive of inner value, independent from social station. However, in introducing these innovations into his lyrics, Walther never alters the fundamental relationship characterizing high courtly love: the lover's eagerness to serve his beloved, that is, his concern for her happiness, her pleasure. Even in the poem 'Unter der linden,' often cited as depicting low courtly love, the fundamental strictures of high courtly love are not violated: the lover waits upon the beloved, who is impressed by the manner in which she is received, he prepares their bed of flowers, the necessary secrecy of the relationship is maintained, and the speaker, the beloved, leaves no doubt about her awareness of his concern for her pleasure. This is in distinct contrast to much of the poetry of Neidhart of Reuenthal, who frequently injects himself, by name, into his verses as the erotic hero, for whom sundry peasant wenches, and their mothers, pine. The relationship of poetic evocation to individualized 'reality', or real individuals, has its parallel in painting and sculpture. The poetry of Reinmar of Hagenau can be identified with the Romanesque perception of 'reality', that of Walther with early Gothic, and the songs of Neidhart with later Gothic art.[10]

The significance of Walther's poetry is not limited, however, to the love lyric, but extends to his *Spruchdichtung*, i.e. gnomic verse. In medieval German literature one distinguishes two types of such verse, the one spoken, the other sung. The latter is a subgenre of lyric poetry, and it is this type of gnomic verse that constitutes a large part of Walther's poetry. The most famous of Walther's *Sprüche* determined the depiction of the poet in the most important collection of medieval German lyric poetry, the Manesse manuscript, which was compiled a century after his lifetime:

Plate 48

> I sat upon a stone,
> leg crossed by leg; thereon
> I put my elbow up
> and in my hand did cup
> one cheek, and chin as well.
> My thoughts upon the problem fell
> of how, on earth, to lead one's life.

> At answers I could not arrive
> how one could manage to possess
> three things of lasting wholesomeness.
> Honour and wealth are two of these,
> but each the other does disease.
> The third thing longed for is God's grace,
> surpassing all, in highest place.
> These three I'd like to have as one:
> Unfortunately it can't be done,
> that wealth and honour in the world entwine
> and with the grace of God combine
> to flow into one heart as one.
> The roads and paths for them are gone.
> For treachery in the ambush hides,
> brute force the travelled roads bestrides,
> while Peace and Justice are grievous hurt.
> The former three abandoned are, unless these two
>   with strength be girt.

The characteristics of Walther's love lyrics are no less noticeable in this didactic plaint of the times and the unattainability of the principal components of the medieval scale of values: *summum bonum, honestum,* and *utile.* The didactic content of the poem, basically matter for a learned, moralistic disquisition, is introduced by the description of de-conventionalized, natural action of the narrator. This introduction not only 'personalizes' an otherwise impersonal 'message', but simultaneously places it into a natural environment consisting of the narrator's natural action. The same tendency to 'personalize' essentially generalized or abstract matter and to render it concrete by investing it with environmental elements belonging to common experience also characterizes Walther's political *Sprüche.* Some of these deal with the relationship between empire and papacy, a relationship in which Walther consistently favours the empire, hurling accusations against the papacy which were once more to gain currency three hundred years later in the writings of Martin Luther.

Figs. 46, 47

Whereas the lyrics of Heinrich of Veldeke (c. 1150– c. 1210) did not exert much influence on the development of the courtly lyric in general, his epic poem, *Eneit*—an adaptation of Vergil's *Aenead* on the basis of the Old French *Roman d'Eneas*—was of great significance for the evolution of the medieval German courtly epic. The narrative matter is here first used as a vehicle for the depiction of courtly behaviour and courtly love. In consonance with this function of the narrative, Lavinia's role, of secondary importance in the *Aenead,* becomes central to Heinrich's poem. But the mock battle, the chivalric play *par excellence,* the joust, and the most crucial of courtly concepts, that of 'aventiure', i.e. adventure, are still unknown to Heinrich. His principal achievement lies in extensive use of dialogue, and the avoidance of impure rhyme, irregular rhythm, and too much regional dialect.

The function of the medieval German courtly epic as vehicle for the elucidation and criticism of courtly ideals becomes evident in the works of Hartmann of Aue (c. 1170– c. 1215). Both of his epic poems, *Erec* and *Iwein*, are directly dependent on the *Erec* and *Yvain* of Chrétien de Troyes. Hartmann, however, has shifted emphases, expanded one part, contracted another, and by this means created works which, in their significance as critiques of courtly civilization, differ considerably from their French models.

Like the courtly lyric, courtly epic poems should not be read with the preconceptions formed by the constant, if subconscious, perception of time and space in post-medieval narrative literature. The graphic arts can again offer an indication of the manner in which these romances of chivalry were read and understood. Perspective, the creation of a realistic visual illusion, plays as little role in painting around 1200 as the creation of a realistic verbal illusion of temporal and spacial relationships in literature.

Fig. 46 Hands freed from mail, mittens at extremity of sleeves. Miniature from the Berlin Eneit *manuscript (after Schultz)*

This does not mean, however, that all literature of this period must be read as allegory.[11] Not all painting of the twelfth and thirteenth centuries can be called allegorical, no matter how loosely the term 'allegory' is used. Critics who maintain that medieval man could only perceive and only express himself allegorically, fail to take into account that arts other than literature are also forms of expression, creating and demanding patterns of perception. Symbolic expression as well as perception governed literature as well as the pictorial arts.[12] A courtly epic, like a lyric poem, must therefore be approached neither as a story of the adventures of a hero tacitly assumed to be human and moving in a three-dimensional world, nor as the basis for the scholastic construction of an allegorical edifice consisting of a *sensus moralis*, a *sensus allegoricus* and a *sensus analogicus*. It has been observed that three-dimensionality—the illusion of depth, of an individual interacting with a realistic environment, being uniquely formed by it and forming it uniquely—play no role in courtly literature. All its knights are pale, equally one-dimensional 'figures'. They serve,

Fig. 47 Chain-mail. Another miniature from the Berlin Eneit *manuscript (after Schultz)*

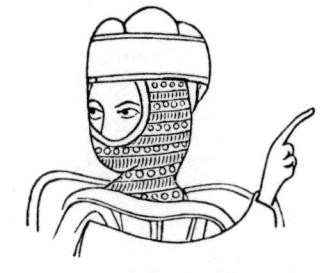

just as do the figures in the lyric, as vehicles for concepts. The story is merely the verbal basis for the construction, not of a pseudo-reality, but of a critical view of 'reality' without the aid of illusionistic depiction.

It is essential, moreover, to distinguish the 'adventures' of the knight in the epics from the modern connotation of the term. An adventure is currently conceived to be an extra-ordinary experience—extraordinary in the sense that it differs from the types of experience which compose the major part of life. It is therefore not conceived as being part of life in general. An 'adventure' is never incorporated in the fabric of life, it always forms an entity apart from 'common' experience. It cannot even be integrated organically in a series of 'adventures': it will always remain one of that series without merging with the other 'adventures', without forming them or being formed by them. In the courtly epic, however, 'adventure' is the very fabric of—not life—but the action of the protagonists. The series of adventures confronting the knight is composed of organically related elements: each is of significance to each of the others. The adventures of the knight, his reactions to each of the problems posed, are the structural segments from which the 'meaning' of the entire work emanates. Unlike the current concept of the term, the adventures in the courtly epic are essential to its structure and not extraordinary as components of the protagonists' action.

All the great Middle High German courtly epics of the end of the twelfth and the beginning of the thirteenth century—the *Erec* (c. 1192) and *Iwein* (c. 1202) of Hartmann of Aue, the *Parzival* (1200–1210) of Wolfram of Eschenbach, and the *Tristan* (c. 1210) of Gottfried of Strassburg—are criticisms of chivalric society and courtly ideals. A short passage from *Iwein* can serve to exemplify the statement of a problem which recurs in varying forms in these epics and which illustrates the fundamental weakness of chivalric ideals. First, the background: Kalogreant, a knight at King Arthur's court, relates how, seek-

The Chivalric Period

ing adventure, he rode out and eventually reached a clearing in a forest. There he saw all sorts of animals, bison and aurochs among them, fighting with one another and making a terrible din. In their midst sat a man who, however, appeared as terrible to Kalogreant as the beasts around him: he was black and bigger than an aurochs. His black hair as well as his beard was matted, his face wrinkled, his huge ears were overgrown with hair, his eyebrows bushy, his nose—as big as that of an ox—short, broad, and hairy, his eyes red, his large mouth revealed the teeth of a boar, and his posture was that of a hunchback. When Kalogreant drew near, this apparent monster rose and approached Kalogreant, who addressed him with considerable trepidation:

> I asked, 'Evil or good—what might you be?'
> He said, 'Who does no harm to me
> shall find me no less friendly, too.'
> 'In that case, I'd be obliged if you
> would tell what creature you might be.'
> 'I am a man, as you can see.'
> 'And what's your calling, tell me then.'
> 'These beasts—I watch over them.'
> 'Have you no fear of them at all?'
> 'They're glad I don't upon them fall.'
> 'Indeed, are *they* afraid of *you*?'
> 'I care for them; in turn, they do
> quake before me as their lord.'
> 'What can your mastery afford
> against their running as their mood
> takes them into field and wood?
> For I can see they're wild indeed,
> unlikely man or his law to heed.
> Without God's help, I doubt it much
> that the power and strength of man be such
> as keep these beasts from running amok

without fetters, bonds, or lock.'
He said, 'My tongue and strength of hand,
my threat and also my command
have filled them with such fear of me,
they tremble before me awfully.
Should someone else, however, dare
to be, as I, in their midst, he'd fare
most terribly, for he'd be lost.'
'If, sir, your anger they fear the most,
then tell them to be kind to me.'
He said, 'No cause for you afraid to be:
They'll harm you not while I'm with you.
But now that I have told you true
what you have deigned to ask of me,
you will, I hope, not impatiently
tell me what you wish to find.
If I can help, I would not mind,
—what needs be done, I'm glad to do.'
I said, 'I'll gladly answer you.
I seek adventure as a knight.'
'Adventure? What is that, I pray?'
'I'll explain it, if I may.
Look upon my weapons here:
I am a knight, and without fear
I ride and seek another knight
who, armed as I, might want to fight.
If he slays me, that's to his praise,
do I slay him, then that does raise
my worth as man o'er what it is.
If, then, adventure such as this
be known to you not far from here,
then don't be silent, let me hear,
direct me to the proper place,
for in wrong directions I might face.'

The Chivalric Period

> He answered thereupon my plea:
> 'If your mind determined be
> to make you seek discomfort great
> and shun a comfortable state
> —in all my life I never heard
> about "adventure" a single word—
> but, all the same, I'll tell you this:
> if risks to your life you hate to miss,
> you needn't enquire further.'

Following the hirsute hunchback's instructions, Kalogreant rides off to find a certain well, and pours water on a stone above it. As a result, the surrounding forest is all but destroyed by a storm. Calm is scarcely restored, when Kalogreant is challenged by a knight, who accuses him of wilfully destroying his forest without cause. In the ensuing joust, Kalogreant is promptly unhorsed and, after taking off his heavy armour, betakes himself home on foot.

The contrast between Kalogreant, the knight, and the deformed creature with whom he converses, emerges not only from Kalogreant's depiction, but also from his description of his reaction to the creature. The latter is made to appear, by Kalogreant, as other than human, perhaps sub-human. Moreover, this monster, primeval in appearance as well as by virtue of its surroundings and its relationship to them, confesses to an utter ignorance of the civilized, chivalric behaviour exemplified by Kalogreant: 'Adventure? What is that, I pray?' This creature represents nothing more strange than a peasant, the embodiment of the very opposite of chivalric ideals. Yet this peasant is revealed as more human than the knight. He plays a constructive, necessary role in his environment: he controls the animals in his charge. Kalogreant is part of no environment: he is an isolated figure, seeking a chance encounter. The peasant's actions are organic to the situation from which they emanate: 'Who does no harm to me/shall find me no less friendly, too.' Kalogreant's actions are gratuitous: 'I ride and seek another knight,/who, armed as I, might want to fight.' Not only is this action unmotivated, it is also purposeless. In the lines 'If he slays me, that's to his praise,/ do I slay him, then that does raise/my worth as man o'er what it is' Kalogreant implies that a man's 'worth' in no way depends upon his performing any useful function. Victory is the sole criterion by which his excellence can be measured and his worth will increase with each successive victorious encounter.

Iwein attempts to follow Kalogreant in this adventure and is successful in slaying his opponent, entering his castle, and eventually marrying his widow. However, he is seduced into continuing his former life as knight-errant by his friend Gawain. His wife grants him a year during which he may seek adventure as he likes. The end of the year comes, but Iwein does not realize it until it is too late. The rest of the epic describes Iwein's gradual conquest of his guilt and disorientation by means of a series of adventures, each of which symbolizes a step on his way to sanity and human society.

In entering the castle of his initial opponent, Iwein sets foot in a world in which responsibility to another plays a dominant role. The widow of his opponent is persuaded to marry him for a very practical reason: who could protect her realm better than the conqueror of her previous protector? In addition to this duty, Iwein has taken upon himself a personal obligation to his wife as a human being. In neglecting the latter, he neglects the former. His consciousness of this neglect, his feeling of guilt, however, indicates that he—unlike Kalogreant—can break out of the ideal chivalric frame of mind, cease his adherence to a form of existence which is unintegrated with others and makes no allowance for human emotions, and take his place as an operative member of human society. Kalogreant cannot even face the challenge of that society. Iwein faces the challenge, enters the realm of responsibility, fails within it, rejects it and is rejected in turn, and finally returns to it after utterly rejecting the unreal, Arthurian, world of chivalry.

The Chivalric Period

Criticism of courtly ideals is already implicit in Hartmann's first epic, *Erec*, written some ten years before *Iwein*. Erec's problem, as it is exemplified in the turning point of this epic, is the opposite of Iwein's. Initially, Erec appears as a knight without a past, without chivalric accomplishment, a neutral figure. Without the performance of actions demonstrating a human purpose, without 'self-consciousness', he passes through several adventures and wins Enite as well as the highest praise of Arthur's court. On the pinnacle of Arthurian perfection, which he had reached by somnambulistic execution of tasks conforming to the bloodless Arthurian dream, catastrophe threatens his existence. Whereas Iwein violates his responsibilities to his wife, Erec forgets his duties as a knight and 'verliget sich', that is, becomes laggard, preferring domestic bliss to the active life of a knight. Enite complains of this, and Erec, ordering her to accompany him in silence as his squire, rides out, seeking adventure. In the course of the ensuing encounters with robbers, evil counts, a dwarf, and giants, Enite, risking death, repeatedly breaks her vow of silence in order to save Erec from impending disaster, and Erec finally saves Enite from the unwanted advances of count Oringles. At this point, a human relationship between the two, surpassing Arthurian ideals, is established.

A different sort of criticism of the courtly ideal is presented by the *Parzival* of Wolfram von Eschenbach. Parzival is taken into the wilderness by his mother in an attempt to save him from the same fate as his father's, who was killed performing the duties of a knight. Parzival must never be allowed to find out what knighthood is. One day, however, he meets three knights in the forest and learns from them of the seat of knighthood at Arthur's court. Intent now on becoming a knight, he leaves his mother, who decks him out in fool's clothing, hoping that ridicule will drive him back to her. On his departure, but without his knowledge, she dies. After some adventures, he arrives at Arthur's court, but although he wins a contest with Ither, the Red Knight, his behaviour on this occasion indicates that he is not ready for knighthood. However, he finds a mentor in Gurnemanz, an old knight, who teaches him all the Compleat Knight needs to know, cautioning him, among other things, against asking unnecessary questions. At the Grail Castle, where Parzival is confronted by a number of baffling ceremonies as well as the sight of the mysteriously ailing Grail King, this advice proves fateful. The human capacity for pity, which Parzival had shown by crying, as a boy, when he had shot birds, as well as the second part of Gurnemanz's advice, to 'let pity be paired with valour', are now submerged by the un-human artificiality of the chivalric ideal: neither the ceremony of the Holy Grail, nor the sufferings of the Grail King elicit questions from him. This adventure is followed by a catastrophe: Parzival is cursed by Kundrie, ambassador from the Grail Castle, in the presence of the knights of Arthur's court. He leaves the court and begins the long journey back from guilt to humanity, from initial defiance of God, to the final admission 'I am a sinful man', with which he identifies himself to the hermit Trevrizent, Parzival's spiritual mentor. Parzival ultimately conquers his disorientation and confusion of human and chivalric values. His humiliation and surrender to God's grace fit him for his ultimate fate: the kingship of the Grail.

Erec and *Parzival* share the same structural formula: the hero's initial goal is Arthur's court, which then serves as the point of departure for his subsequent adventures. For Iwein, the court of Arthur is the initial point of departure. All three, however, share a bipartite structure: the search for the goal and its unconscious achievement is followed by the catastrophe, which gives rise to the second search for a goal and the conscious transcendence of a purely Arthurian solution. This second search, basically a search for the self, is initiated by the hero's relinquishment of 'vröude', courtly gregariousness, the very essence of Arthurian courtliness, and his flight from society. Alone in the wilderness he must find himself, make his way back to human society, in order to transcend, with the self-knowledge thus acquired, the self-deluding Arthurian dream, and return to reality. The structure of these and other courtly epics is, in its essence, comparable to that of a Gothic cathedral. Just as all architectural aspects of a cathedral emanate from one basic geometrical form, all structural aspects of the courtly epic are extrapolations of one structural pattern.

The *Tristan und Isolt* of Gottfried of Strassburg is an epic of an altogether different type. In a programmatic prologue, the narrator —not to be identified, as in the case of some primitive literary criticism, with the author—distinguishes between two types of men: those who want nothing but pleasure, and those—the 'noble hearts'—who are not only willing, but eager to embrace the bad with the good, the unpleasant with the pleasant, as two sides of the same coin. It is to the latter that the narrator addresses his tale.

Tristan is orphaned and reared by his father's marshal, Rual, who sees to it that the boy receives the best that education has to offer, both in learning and chivalric training, as well as in the acquisition of the social graces. Abducted by merchants, he is set free on the coast of Cornwall and makes his way to Tintagel, to the court of king Mark, where, much admired, he quickly becomes the royal favourite. He rids the kingdom of the oppressor Morolt, but is wounded and must go to Ireland to be healed by Morolt's sister, Isolt. Incognito, he becomes tutor to her daughter Isolt. Upon his return to Tintagel, Mark resolves to marry young Isolt, and Tristan is sent back to Ireland as his ambassador. After several adventures, including Isolt's discovery of his true identity as the slayer of her uncle, he succeeds in his mission. On the voyage back to Cornwall Tristan and Isolt—the former behaving with great propriety toward Isolt, the latter not hiding her antipathy toward him and her fate—both accidentally drink of a love potion destined for Isolt and Mark. They attempt to fight its effects, but to no avail. At Mark's court they are involved in a series of adventures and ruses by means of which the two lovers attempt to satisfy their individual desires, while at the same time playing their social roles at court, Isolt as queen, Tristan as royal favourite. Mark, with some reluctance, faces the realities of the situation and exiles them. In the wilderness they live in the love-grotto, leading a life of perfect harmony. When Mark, fearing that he had been unjust in banning them, allows them to return to court, they accept his invitation, whereupon they again face the conflict between their individual desires and the demands of society. Eventually the true state of affairs can no longer be concealed, and Tristan is exiled. After some adventures and much vacillation, he accepts the love of Isolde of the White Hands. Here Gottfried's poem breaks off.

The epic is explicitly presented as a problem piece: many, says the narrator in the prologue, have told the story of Tristan and Isolt, but only Thomas of Brittany (or Britain) has told it correctly. He therefore uses Thomas' version—of which only a short fragment is transmitted—as a basis. The theme did indeed present the courtly poet with a major problem, for it was intractable in terms of courtly ideals. Chrétien, author of a *Tristan* which is now lost, refers to the love of Tristan and Isolt as dishonourable (*Cligès*, 5250 ff). This love is altogether different from courtly love: it is neither sought by service, nor bestowed as reward. Tristan and Isolt accidentally, unintentionally and therefore without guilt, 'fall in love'. They do not voluntarily become parties to a socially sanctioned contract in which each has his duties and his rights; they are overpowered by a personal, human emotion. The fact that this emotion befalls them accidentally emphasizes its human nature: it can occur to anyone, at any time. A denial of this emotion is a denial of humanity. Such a denial, however, is exactly what courtly society, the social order, exemplified by Mark and his court, demands. To Mark, Isolt is not an individual, she is his queen. He is primarily concerned, not with her feelings, but with his 'êre', his reputation. Flight from society, open defiance, or subversion of the social order, are unacceptable solutions to the dilemma confronting the lovers, since they are no solutions: society is here to stay, the social order is a necessary order, and only one who desires nothing but pleasure, the 'ignoble heart', is sufficiently unrealistic to refute this. The 'noble heart', however, accepts the unpleasant with the pleasant. The lovers, therefore, embrace the tension between their human emotion on the one hand and the demands of the social order on the other: their return from the erotic paradise of the love-grotto to Mark's court is voluntary. At the moment, however, when Tristan surrenders to convenience and accepts the love of Isolde of the White Hands, he ceases to be a 'noble heart'. But this concept of 'noble hearts', as it is set forth in the prologue, cannot be taken at its face value in the manner of most critics. The entire poem is fraught with hitherto unnoticed irony, which extends even to this programmatic concept: Tristan's parents were anything but 'noble hearts', neither were Tristan and Isolt before drinking the potion, nor Isolt afterwards, as is illustrated by her behaviour toward her devoted lady-in-waiting Brangaene. The function of the epic as criticism of courtly society is obvious, but to read it as an unsophisticated, one-directional 'message' is to read it with one eye closed. Once the reader is aware of the function of irony in the poem he will recognize that the 'message' itself, and even the ironist, are not immune from it.

The *Nibelungenlied* (*c.* 1200) occupies a unique position in medieval German literature. Its narrative matter belongs to heroic rather than courtly poetry and emanates from the age of the migrations, from the fourth to the seventh century. It is the tale of Siegfried, the all but invincible hero, his coming to the court of Gunther, king of the Burgundians, at Worms, to sue for the hand of Gunther's sister, Kriemhild. As part of the bargain, Siegfried agrees to help Gunther win the all but invincible Brünhild. The necessary ruse of appearing as vassal to king Gunther rather than as the independent, mighty hero which he really is, places Siegfried in a dangerous position at Gunther's court, which ultimately leads to his murder. Brünhild, symbol of impregnability, can only be conquered by the strongest, i.e. Siegfried, who does conquer her, while Gunther *appears* to do so. Only Siegfried, Gunther, his adviser Hagen, and Dancwart, Hagen's brother, know this secret. Kriemhild guesses it, for Siegfried gives her the belt and ring, which he had wrested from Brünhild. Brünhild *appears* to be the wife of the mightiest man, who in fact owes her to the strength of one who *seems* to be his vassal. Siegfried, as the symbol and paragon of individual strength, is no threat to the power of Gunther—as long as this secret is kept. Kriemhild, however, thirsts for independent power.[13] Therefore it is essential for Kriemhild, as the wife of the only man who could subdue Brünhild, to assert her superiority over the latter. What must remain secret for the sake of Gunther, must be made known for the sake of Kriemhild. Kriemhild, therefore, picks a quarrel over precedence with Brünhild and publicly displays her ring and belt as evidence for her assertions. Although Siegfried protests his innocence, maintaining that he had not, as Kriemhild claimed, robbed Brünhild of her maidenhood, the damage is done: it is clear to all that, whatever the truth may be, Siegfried had something to do with Gunther's winning of Brünhild. Gunther's sudden decision to forego the public oath demanded by him and proffered by Siegfried, asseverating the latter's innocence, indicates his awareness of the implications of such an oath. A shadow is thus cast over Gunther's prowess, which can only be removed by the removal of the figure casting the shadow: Siegfried. Hagen therefore kills him and thus restores Gunther's prominence: 'now', he says, 'there are none who dare challenge us' (st. 993).[14] In order to prevent Kriemhild from taking revenge for her husband's murder, the Burgundians deprive her of Siegfried's treasure. In the course of time, however, Kriemhild marries Etzel (Attila), king of the Huns, and uses the power she gains thereby to avenge

The Chivalric Period

Siegfried's death: she invites her brothers and Hagen to Etzel's court. After a series of bloody battles, none save Etzel himself, his vassal Dietrich of Bern and Dietrich's comrade-in-arms Hildebrand survive.

Although both parts of the *Nibelungenlied*—the story of Siegfried's prowess and death, and the account of Kriemhild's revenge—consist of heroic narrative matter, the epic, as it is transmitted, must not be mistaken for an heroic epic. The distinction between the subject matter which went into it and the recorded poem must be kept clearly in mind. The former is part of the heroic narrative tradition and was transmitted orally; the latter, the *Nibelungenlied*, as we know it, is a poem composed by a literate, courtly poet around 1200, whose work achieved great popularity with the readers of *Parzival, Tristan,* and the poems of Hartmann. The fact that the transmitted poem exhibits varying densities of oral formulaic phrases and other characteristics of orally composed and transmitted poetry, reveals that the writing poet chose this oral narrative material as a basis for his written composition presumably because it was well known and popular, and because it suited his purpose. His purpose, however—if a slight digression into the 'intentional fallacy' be permitted in order to counter a widely held view—cannot be identified with that of the oral poet. A reading of the *Nibelungenlied*, for instance, as a depiction of exemplary heroism, as a paean of praise in honour of Siegfried and the 'old heroic virtues', is at variance with the text of the poem as well as with its clearly marked destination for a courtly audience. If on the other hand we take the poem to exemplify certain types of heroism, that, in a supra-individual sense, represent well-defined cultural epochs, and evaluate these types to the detriment of the culture of their day, then we are projecting a modern form of historical consciousness onto a medieval context.

In short, the transmitted *Nibelungenlied* is to be read, not as its narrative matter suggests, but as its text indicates, as a courtly epic. To be sure, it is sometimes difficult—far more difficult than in the case of a pure courtly epic—to view the actions of the protagonists, particularly those of Hagen, as those of figures rather than of 'characters'. Their undeniable three-dimensionality repeatedly tempts the reader to perceive these figures and their actions in modern novelistic terms. However, the structural inconsistencies in characterization, e.g. Siegfried's two youthful periods—the one courtly, the other heroic—the double characterizations of Gunther and Brünhild, the strange behaviour of Dietrich, leave no alternative but to approach these 'characters' as figures.[15] The literary historical environment of the *Nibelungenlied* only underscores the necessity for this view, which is dictated by the poem itself.

At issue is the conflict—of political significance in the eleventh and twelfth centuries—between two forms of power: *de facto* and *de jure* might. At the first meeting of the two protagonists—Siegfried and Gunther at Worms—the programme is clearly stated. Siegfried wants to conquer Gunther's realm in single combat against the latter: whoever is victorious deserves to rule over the possessions of the conquered as well as his own. Gunther's court is aghast at the proposal: their right to the realm is legitimate and not to be put to such a random test. Only the continuity of their power can assure order in a society which is far more complicated than that which gave birth to Siegfried. The Burgundians view Siegfried, however, not as a necessary enemy, but as a very useful potential ally, and are successful in dissuading him from his initial intention. As a symbol of personal capability, he is incorporated into the courtly social order represented by Gunther's court by means of his marriage to Kriemhild, who, as symbol of illegitimate striving for power, poses a danger to the social order and, at the same time, can welcome this marriage as a step toward her own independence. Gunther, representative of legitimacy, does not *need* to be, but must *appear* to be the most capable individual: hence his marriage to Brünhild, who can only be won by Siegfried. When appearances are threatened by Kriemhild's revelation of the facts, Siegfried again poses a threat to Burgundian power. After Siegfried's elimination, both Kriemhild and her brothers seek to exercise the type of power represented by Siegfried in order to attain the unattainable: the source of Siegfried's power. Kriemhild seeks vengeance and Siegfried's treasure, which her brothers and Hagen have taken from her. The Burgundians play a defensive role: they refuse to give up the treasure. The issue of the treasure is not, as a primitive form of literary criticism would have it, a motif left over from older versions of the epic, which the poet 'could not eliminate'; it is the very crux of the poem's argument at this point. The treasure of Siegfried, the Nibelungen hoard, consists of three parts: the gold which was sunk in the Rhine by the Burgundians, the sword which Hagen carries, and the magic cloak. It is the magic cloak which is of primary significance, for this is the source, not only of Siegfried's power of making himself invisible, but also of his superhuman strength. The latter attribute constitutes his power, his competence as an individual. But the magic cloak is now unattainable—it vanished at Siegfried's death. Unattainable, likewise, is the type of power which it symbolized. Siegfried's own failure in the context of the stable courtly society of the Burgundians has demonstrated, moreover, that such power in these circumstances is at best of no avail and at worst dangerous—unless it is coupled with a legitimacy whereby the continuity of social order is ensured.

During the two centuries preceding the composition of the *Nibelungenlied*, governmental administration had become increasingly complex. All of western and central Europe was more densely populated, the population ever more dependent on extensive trade, so that the very existence of society depended on a continuity of power which only a union of competence and legitimacy could assure. Competence alone—the ability to obtain or retain *de facto* power—is governed by events: at any moment the competence of one may be challenged by that of another. Legitimacy, of whatever sort—whether the criterion be heredity or the choice of princes—must, of course, be accompanied by competence, without being overshadowed by it. The competence to defend legitimacy is sufficient, the possession of omnipotence is beside the point, and the will to test competence is destructive to society. The spectacle of the constant conflicts between emperor and princes, with competence and legitimacy all too often contending with each other and endangering the survival of the social order at every turn, is reflected in the elucidation of this problem in the *Nibelungenlied*. Together with the gnomic poetry of Walther, the *Nibelungenlied* testifies to the clash of the highly developed Hohenstaufen state with its competitors for legitimacy, and the dangers this confrontation held for the fabric of German society.

Chapter IV

Social Chaos and Cultural Change

WITH THE DEATH of Conrad IV in 1254 the Hohenstaufen empire came to an end. The death of the former anti-king William of Holland in 1256 during a campaign against the Frisians increased the factionalism which was already rife throughout Germany. The candidate of the Pope and of the archbishops of Cologne and Mainz, the most powerful of German ecclesiastics, was Richard, earl of Cornwall, brother of Henry III of England. Richard fitted the requisites of the archbishop of Cologne for the German crown: sufficiently rich to support its dignity, he was yet too weak to threaten the power of the princes. The opposition, led by the archbishop of Trier and the dukes of Brandenburg, Saxony, and the king of Bohemia, supported king Alfonso X of Castile. The former was proclaimed in January 1257, the latter in March of the same year, both in Frankfurt. King Alfonso, called 'the Wise', never set foot on German soil. King Richard, however, arrived in Aachen in May 1257 and, in return for 12,000 pounds sterling, received the crown from the archbishop of Cologne. In the course of his progress up the Rhine during the summer he wasted his substance to such a degree that he had to sell some of his holdings in England in order to replenish his treasury—but to no avail: at Basel his supporters left him. He returned in 1260, but accomplished nothing.

A third name mentioned as candidate for the German crown was that of the son of Conrad IV, Conradin, who was now five years old. Conradin became the final victim of the Sicilian policy pursued by his ancestors. At a rumour of Conradin's death, Manfred, the son of Frederick II and regent for Conradin, was persuaded to take the crown of Sicily himself. The papal policy toward a Hohenstaufen Sicily remained unchanged after the

Fig. 48

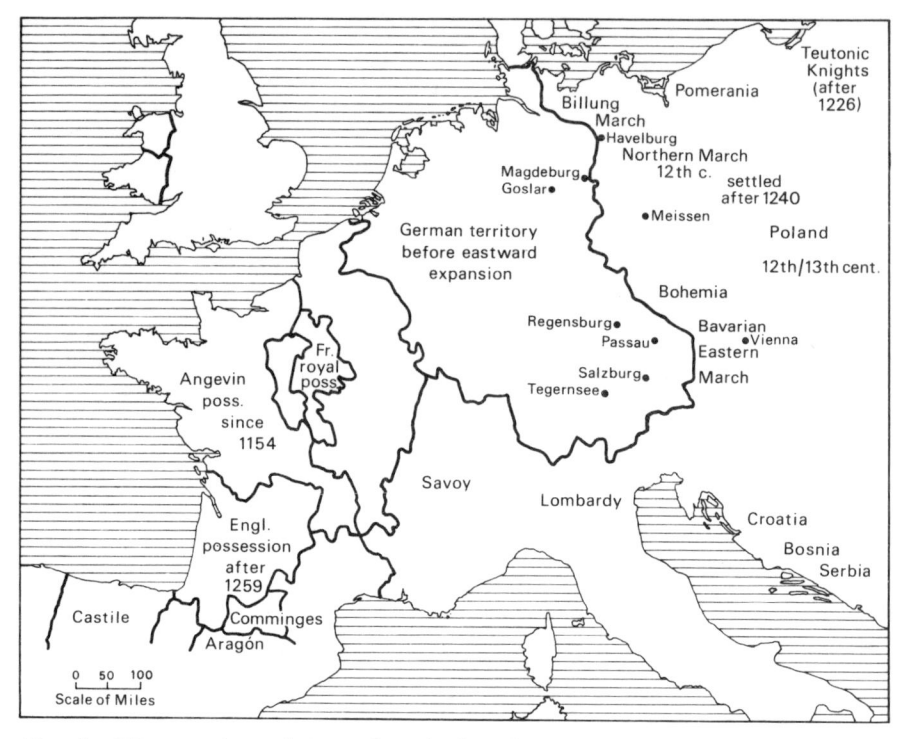

Fig. 48 Western and central Europe from the eleventh to the end of the thirteenth century

death of Innocent IV. Urban IV renewed the interdict and attempted to prompt count Charles of Anjou, brother of king Louis IX of France, to act as secular executor of the ecclesiastical curse. Pope Clement IV, Urban's successor, finally reached an agreement with Charles, according to which the latter received hereditary rights to Sicily in return for a total of 8,000 ounces of gold annually in addition to a large payment immediately after the conquest; if, however, payment of the monthly fee became six months overdue, Charles' rights to his kingdom would be rescinded; if no payment were made for two months, the realm of Sicily would be subject to the papal interdict. Charles accepted these conditions. At the battle of Benevento in February 1266, he gave orders, against all chivalric tradition, to spear the horses of

Fig. 49 Miniature from the manuscript Alexandri Minoritae Apocalypsis explicata, *Universitätsbibl., Breslau (after Schultz)*

Manfred's knights, and thereby won the day. Encouraged by remnants of Hohenstaufen adherents, Conradin went to Italy with an army of about 10,000 men, was defeated at the battle of Scurcola on August 22, 1268, captured a few days later, and executed in Naples on October 29, 1268, aged sixteen. The end of the Hohenstaufen dynasty signified also the end of the connection between the German monarchy and Italy, as well as the final defeat of the empire in its struggle with the papacy.

The victors in Germany were the princes, who now emerged as their own masters. The extinction, moreover, of several great dynasties left many petty nobles without feudal superiors and free to extend their domains by any means and in any direction. Similarly, imperial *ministeriales* converted their offices into feudal holdings. As a consequence, Germany in general and the Hohenstaufen domains in particular became utterly fragmented, a 'land with so many lords that it was in essence lordless' (Barraclough). The holdings of the nobility underwent shifts, which were occasioned either by assertion of simple might of one against another, or by redivision of lands such as that undertaken by the houses of Wittelsbach, Brandenburg, Saxony, and the Welfs. Henceforth seven great princes exercised the right of imperial election: the archbishops of Mainz, Cologne, and Trier, the king of Bohemia, the duke of Saxony, the margrave of Brandenburg, and the count palatine of the Rhine.

The need for order was most urgently felt by the cities and led to more rapid formation of city leagues. The most formidable of these alliances was the Hanseatic League, which developed in part from the treaty of 1241 between Hamburg and Lübeck, and was designed to secure the commercial traffic of these cities between the North Sea and the Baltic. Of no less significance for the development of this league were the associations of German merchants in foreign countries. The oldest and most powerful of these guilds of German merchants was in London, where the merchants from Cologne were granted royal protection by Henry II in 1157. Already king Aethelred had granted the *homines imperatoris*, the emperor's men, 'good laws'. The German commercial settlement in London was the centre of German commerce with Central Europe. A similar association of merchants in Wisby on Gotland dominated trade with the Baltic area and Russia. By the end of the thirteenth century, the Hanseatic League embraced, in addition to Hamburg, Lübeck, and Cologne, the cities of Wismar, Rostock, Brandenburg, Berlin-Kölln, Frankfurt a. d. Oder, Soest, Münster, Minden, Danzig, and many others. Besides clearing the North Sea and the Baltic of pirates and preserving the commercial privileges of its members, the Hanseatic League was instrumental in maintaining political and social order within its member cities, as well as standardizing commercial law, coinage, and weight. The League was supported by contributions levied upon the member cities, and its interests were protected by soldiery and ships provided by them according to their means.

The Rhenish city league was founded in July 1254 at the prompting of Arnold Walpod, a rich merchant of Mainz. It

Fig. 50

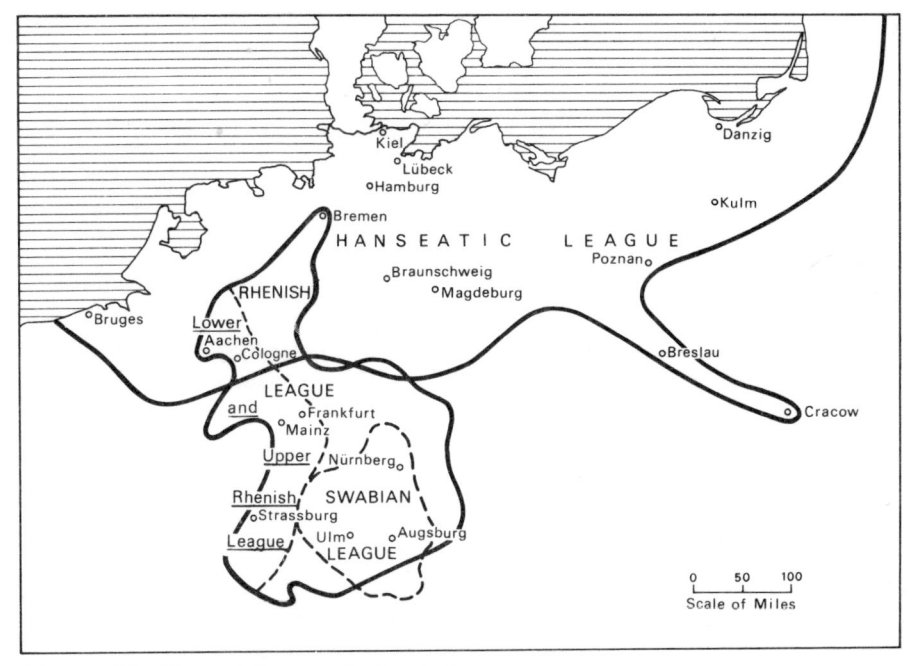

Fig. 50   The Hanseatic League and other city leagues

comprised over fifty bishoprics, archbishoprics, and cities, among which Cologne and Basel were pre-eminent. The principal purpose of this league was the preservation of civil order. The success of these leagues led to the establishment of similar confederations, the most famous of which was the Swabian city league, founded on November 20, 1331 at the instigation of emperor Ludwig the Bavarian. Both the Hanseatic League and the Rhenish city league fulfilled the dual function of maintaining order and furthering commerce. Their success in the former during the Interregnum was responsible for their effectiveness in the latter during the centuries which followed. The Rhenish league with its relatively limited objectives dissolved in the middle of the fifteenth century, whereas the Hanseatic League survived effectively until the seventeenth, nominally until the nineteenth century.

The towns now assumed crucial socio-economic significance. The rate of urbanization had increased slowly during the twelfth, and more rapidly in the thirteenth century. It has been estimated that approximately 3,000 market-towns existed in Germany by the fourteenth century, and that the distance between them was no more than a four to eight hours' journey. Many of these towns, however, remained little more than villages, even though they possessed city charters. The largest German city in the thirteenth century was Cologne with about 35,000 inhabitants —approximately the size of London at the time. In general, one can distinguish three different types of cities, according to their socio-economic function: the market-towns, inhabited for the most part by farmers, artisans and small merchants active in the local agrarian economy; commercial cities, the citizens of which engaged primarily in crafts, supplying a relatively large area with their products and taking part in international commerce to a limited extent; and the great mercantile cities, which were the bases for international commerce. The latter comprised not only some of the largest, but also many relatively small cities.

A city could belong to one of two possible political categories: it was either a *Reichsstadt*, an imperial city, and was directly subject to the emperor, or it was a *Landesstadt* and subject to the local magnate. The municipal officials were almost exclusively members of the city patriciate, the richest of the mercantile families. The basis of power was no longer the possession of land —although some members of the urban patriciate were of the nobility—but mercantile success. Consequently, the composition of the urban patriciate was constantly changing; very few patrician families retained their power for more than five or six generations. Many lost their wealth, others merged with the aristocracy either by marriage or through extensive acquisitions of land. The purchase of land by the rich burgher was not only a form of capital investment, but also a means of increasing his social prestige. The boundary between the merchant class and

Social Chaos and Cultural Change

the aristocracy was always fluid and the transition from one to the other was aided in many cases by the relative poverty of the landed aristocracy.

Non-patrician merchants, like craftsmen, formed guilds. In the Hanseatic cities there were companies of merchants trading, respectively, with England, Flanders, and Russia. These merchants were distinguished from the patriciate only by their lesser wealth. From their ranks the patriciate was replenished.

The majority of the population of the cities consisted of craftsmen. At the end of the fourteenth century, craftsmen, organized in guilds, constituted fifty to sixty per cent of the population of Frankfurt, forty-three per cent of the citizenry of the Hanseatic city of Lübeck. Below the craftsmen in the social scale, and generally without the rights of citizens, were the plebeians, the non-propertied masses of the sick and the old, widows, orphans, servants.

The cities were governed by municipal councils consisting, for the most part, of the patriciate. In the course of time, these councils assumed many of the functions of feudal lords and often actively defended the welfare of the city against their encroachments. In exercising centralized power over a mercantile society, the councils of medieval towns anticipated the function of the state of the fifteenth century. The towns were thus socio-economic as well as political foreign bodies in the surrounding feudal fabric of agrarian society.

Conflicts between the populations of the cities and the nobility were frequent and often bloody. The burghers of Cologne, Mainz, Strassburg, Würzburg, Halle, Speyer, Augsburg, and many other cities, fought embittered battles against their feudal lords for new privileges, often the right to elect their council without interference from them. Gradually some cities extended their power over the surrounding countryside, strengthened their fortifications, and were able to put efficient armies into the field. Instead of taking full advantage of the considerable power of the cities against the nobility, Frederick II supported the princes against them, and thus contributed to the political chaos of the Interregnum.

The demand for the products of urban economy constantly increased during the thirteenth century. Methods of production were steadily improved, calling for ever more specialization: a census of Nuremberg in 1363 reveals 1217 master artisans active in fifty different crafts. The use of the overshot waterwheel led to increased productivity of foundries, the spinning wheel complemented the fulling mill; the vice, the pole-lathe, and the slewing-crane, the utilization of optic lenses, the construction of seaworthy, high-pooped vessels, and the manufacture of paper contributed significantly to increased production and trade.

Mining benefited from rapid advances in tool-manufacture and contributed to the increase of export trade. Silver was mined on the Rammelsberg near Goslar, in Carinthia, Tyrol, Bohemia, and Moravia; iron ore was found in Styria, Carinthia, and Rhenish-Westphalia, copper in Mansfeld, and gold in the Black Forest, in the *Fichtelgebirge* and the Tauern mountains. In the thirteenth and fourteenth centuries German mines supplied all of continental western Europe with silver, copper, and gold.

German exports, initially concentrated on the older commercial centres of northern Italy and Flanders, expanded in the latter part of the thirteenth and the fourteenth century to embrace the Mediterranean area and the Scandinavian countries. The export of wheat increased markedly during this period, and an average of 1250 tons of luxury goods crossed the St Gotthard pass annually. Among imports, cattle from Frisia, Denmark, Poland and Hungary, and cotton from Sicily and Cyprus played a large role. The latter was destined mainly for Upper Germany, where it was converted into retailable forms; oriental silks were likewise worked in Upper Germany and in the Rhineland, hemp and flax in Westphalia, English wool in the Rhineland and Polish wool in the Upper Lausitz.

Fig. 51

Fig. 51   Silk, Germ. Museum, Nuremberg (after Schultz)

The commercial traffic engendered by the productivity of the relatively well-governed towns and overland trade with foreign countries were continuously endangered by the social chaos prevailing in the countryside. The disruption of feudal order placed countless knights, even holders of a single castle, in an independent position. With the relative decrease in the value of land and the increase in the value of money the caravans of merchants on the roads and their ships on the rivers, became objects of attraction for the robber-barons. The countryside, particularly along the Rhine and the Danube, was dotted with their strongpoints, toll-gates, and navigational obstacles designed to aid in the extortion of money or goods from the merchant as the price of his passage. There was no law which could provide shelter to the merchant. He had to be prepared either to pay heavy sums to the robber-barons along the way as ransom for himself and his goods, or have his caravan accompanied by an armed convoy.

Obviously, this state of affairs could not be allowed to continue indefinitely. The effects of economic and social instability gradually forced even the great princes to consider taking steps to restore some sort of central authority. Finally the loss of revenues prompted Pope Gregory X to insist that they appoint an emperor, threatening to appoint one himself if they failed to do so. In Frankfurt-am-Main, on September 29, 1273, the princes elected Rudolf, count of Habsburg, to the imperial throne. The choice conformed to the princes' policy of electing a candidate of sufficient wealth but little power. In the latter consideration, however, they were to be sorely disappointed.

Fig. 52

The literature of the period reflected social and political developments from the decline of courtly civilization in the 1230's to the chaos of the Interregnum. The lyrics of Neidhart of Reuenthal and Ulrich of Liechtenstein (d. 1275) testify, in two divergent ways, to the passing of the poetry of courtly love. The songs of the former flaunted every stricture of the genre (cf. p. 128), the

Fig. 52 Tomb of Rudolf of Habsburg in the cathedral of Speyer (after Schultz)

verses of the latter celebrated the tradition, long since petrified and only half understood by the poet, in a formally exemplary, but thematically forced manner. In addition, Ulrich, judge and prefect of the duchy of Styria, wrote the first autobiography in the German language, his *Frauendienst*. The hold which courtly ideals and their surrounding myths exercised over him is demonstrated by his bizarre journeys of 1227 from Venice to Bohemia, clad as Dame Venus, and of 1240, garbed as King Arthur. The knights whom he encountered on the latter escapade seem to have gone along with this proto-Quixote in the service of his Dulcinea, and were duly accepted by him as members of the Round Table. Both of these poets wrote before the Interregnum, but the two directions in the development of lyric poetry indicated by their works continue to be represented. Following the formal adherence to classical *Minnesang* exemplified by Ulrich of Liechtenstein were Conrad of Würzburg and the young king Conradin. The direction in which Neidhart had steered the lyric was represented, above all, by Steinmar of Klingenau, whose verses parody the courtly love lyric: the lover's heart yearns for the beloved like a pig in a poke, a lover's plaint ends in union with the beloved on the straw, and a *Tagelied* or *aubade* begins with the peasant lovers being awakened by the call of the cowherd.[1]

In gnomic verse the work of Freidank is exemplary of bourgeois didacticism. His extremely popular *Bescheidenheit,* i.e. *discretio,* knowledge of what is right, was written *c.* 1230.

The age of chivalry, however, is left well behind in the work of that very prolific and versatile writer, Der Stricker. True, this wandering entertainer defers—rather mechanically and without much success—to the courtly tradition in modernizing the *Rolandslied* in his epic *Karl,* in his Arthurian epic *Daniel vom blühenden Tal* and his *Frauenehre*. More significant, however, are his achievements in the genres of the novelistic verse-tale and gnomic verse. In the former, the tales of *Pfaffe Amis,* the tonsured pre-Eulenspiegel rascal plays his tricks in a realistic, recognizable environment. In the latter, Der Stricker eschews generalities, pointedly condemns the lords and ridicules courtly love.

The political and social turmoil of the Interregnum is, of course, most clearly reflected in gnomic verse. The *Sprüche* of Friedrich of Sunnenburg and the Marner are particularly vehement in their condemnation of contemporary evils; the latter's despair echoes in the imprecation 'God forbid that my children grow up!' In general, these verses are no longer formulations of a courtly ethic. The standpoints represented are bourgeois, religious-didactic, and of wide popular appeal.

Fig. 53

The courtly epic, like the lyric, developed also in two directions. Rudolf of Ems (d. *c.* 1252) produced conservatively courtly epics in his *Wilhelm von Orlens* and *Alexander*. In his courtly legend *Der gute Gerhard,* however, the hero is a merchant of Cologne, and the thematic tradition of the romance of chivalry is applied to him. Rudolf's crowning achievement is a rhymed chronicle of the world. A decade after Rudolf's death, Conrad of Würzburg (d. 1287) wrote verse novellas and legends, some of which, in their relationship to the classical courtly tradition, are reminiscent of the works of Ulrich of Liechtenstein: they constitute an attempt to revive that tradition. Frequently, however, the impossibility of this undertaking seems to have become obvious to the poet, who was led to oppose the use of courtly motifs contrapuntally with his own view of the world. In his *Goldene Schmiede* and the *Trojanerkrieg,* an epic fragment of some 10,000 lines, Conrad created manneristic models, mingling conceits with erudition, for an entire generation of imitators.

About 1250 a poet strongly influenced by the *Nibelungenlied* composed the epic *Kudrun* on the basis of the orally transmitted heroic songs of Hilde and her daughter Kudrun. The epic is in three parts: a brief account of the abduction of Hagen, son of the king of Ireland, by a griffin, and his return; a longer story of the abduction of Hagen's daughter, Hilde, at the behest of Hetel,

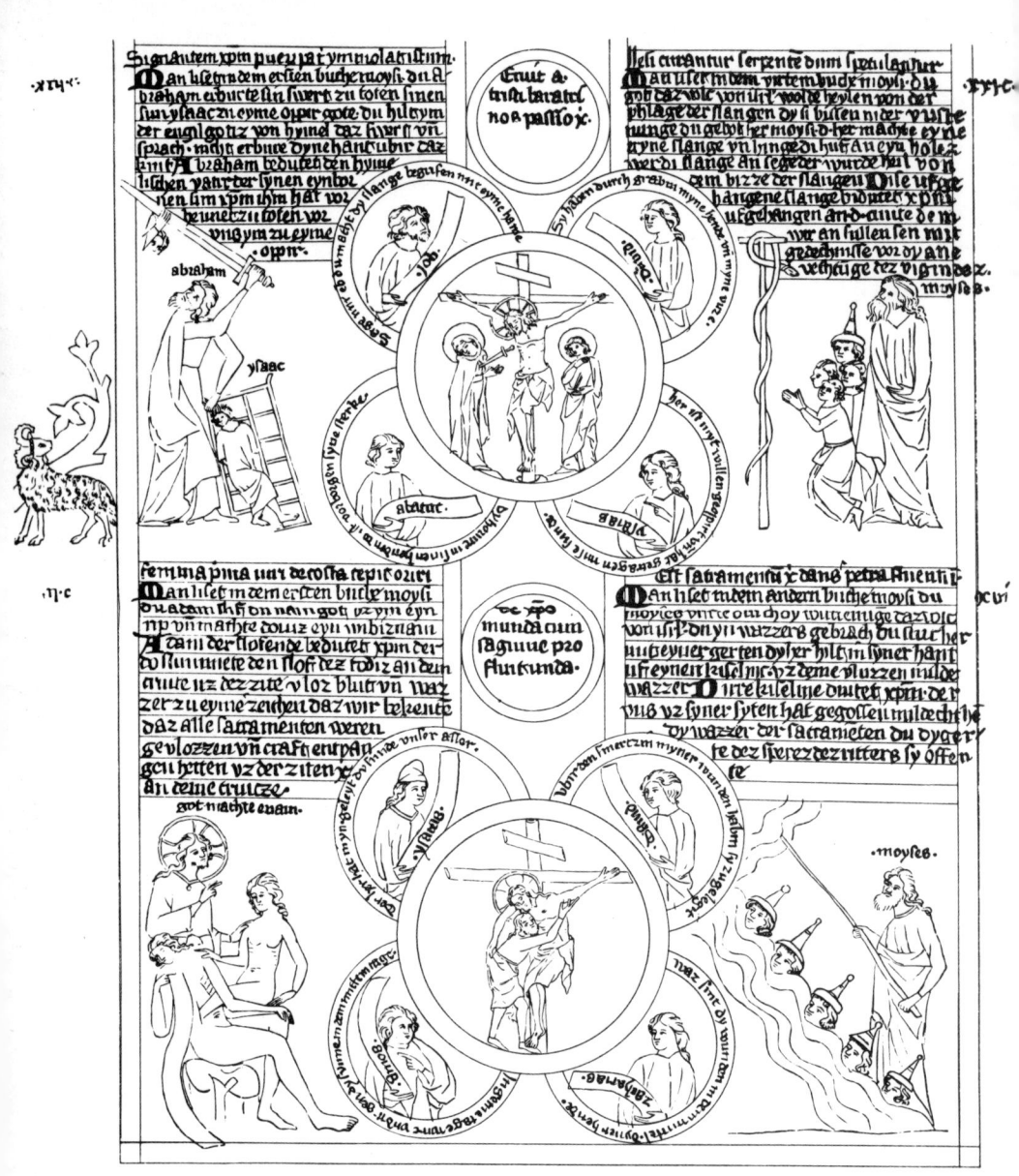

Fig. 53   Crucifixion of Christ in a Biblia pauperum of about 1300. Bibl. d. Lyceums, Konstanz (after Kraus). The illustrated 'Bibles for the poor in spirit', i.e. the populace at large, presented episodes from the Old Testament juxtaposed with those of the New Testament

Social Chaos and Cultural Change

king of Norway; and the main narrative, dealing with the abduction of Kudrun, daughter of Hetel and Hilde, by Hartmut of Normandy, the pursuit of the Normans by Hetel's army, Kudrun's steadfastness while in Norman hands, and her rescue by an army led by her brother and her betrothed. The epic ends with general forgiveness on all sides and a quadruple marriage. In all probability the dominant theme of patience in suffering and eventual forgiveness in this epic is to be viewed as an answer to the second part of the *Nibelungenlied*; the *Kudrun*, in short, can be interpreted as, at least in part, an anti-*Nibelungenlied*. The significant point in such a view is the necessary presupposition that the *Nibelungenlied* was no longer read as a courtly epic at the time of the composition of *Kudrun*, but as a 'story' with a moral. This assumption is borne out by the text of *Kudrun* itself, which, contrary to the courtly epic, is more concerned with three-dimensionality and the emotional consistency of its characters than with any conceptual content or the structural function of figures as vehicles for concepts. As in the case of the lyric and the courtly epic proper, realism tended to displace the components of the courtly tradition: heroes no longer merely perform the actions which mark them as heroes, they are now also human beings, experiencing common physical needs and serving as the butt of ladies' laughter. In such later compositions as *Biterolf* and the *Rosengarten* the perception of heroic material as purely narrative matter, as simply a 'story', becomes unmistakably clear. Traditional motifs of the heroic epic are linked together and the traditional heroes, such as Siegfried, Dietrich, Hildebrand, Gunther, and Hagen, are played out against each other.

By far the most realistic literary production of the 1250's was the satirical poem *Meier Helmbrecht* by Werner der Gärtner. Helmbrecht, the farmer's son, leaves his peasant's existence behind in order to become a knight. He falls in with robber-barons and learns knighthood from them, i.e. toping, plundering, and whoring. On a visit to his parents he shows off his pseudocourtliness by flinging about snatches of French, Latin, and Dutch, and manages to win his sister over to the life he leads by getting her married to one of his comrades. When the robbers fall into the hands of the beadles of the local magnate, Helmbrecht, blinded and maimed, is the sole survivor. His father rejects him, and the peasants finally hang him in retribution for his misdeeds.

The development of a strong tradition of popular preaching during the latter part of the thirteenth century is certainly not unrelated to the prevailing social disorders. The sermons of the Franciscan Berthold of Regensburg (c. 1215-1272) are of particular significance. Concerned mainly with the sins of heresy, superstition, and avarice, he excoriated individual sinners present at the sermons. But far more important than the passionate outbursts themselves is the rich array of rhetorical devices which gives form to the content of the sermons. Prose in the vernacular is beginning to be conceived of as a form adequate for the expression of other than mundane matters.

The visions of the mystic Mechthild of Magdeburg (d. 1282) testify to the increasing use of prose as a vehicle for the conscious formulation of ideas and emotions. Her descriptions of the envelopment of her soul by the 'flowing light of the Godhead', the ecstasy of the mystic union and similar erotic experiences, are suitably worked into the prose narrative with the aid of traditional patterns of expression from the Song of Songs and the courtly love lyric. In short, components of the lyric, rhetorical devices of every sort, now came to be systematically used in vernacular prose as its evocative possibilities were explored. Prose became ever more popular and, in the course of the fourteenth and fifteenth centuries, replaced the rhymed narrative in popular favour to such an extent, that the material of classical Middle High German epics appeared in prose adaptations. Prose translations and the works of the great mystics of the fourteenth century, Eckhart, Tauler, and Seuse, created the means for the development of a variety of prose styles.[2]

Social Chaos and Cultural Change

The increase of realism in literature, the stress on matter rather than form, the development of prose, and the rise of urban culture, trade, and the bourgeoisie are not unrelated phenomena. The development of trade and the steadily growing complexity of governmental administration on all levels occasioned an ever increasing demand for literacy. This literacy, moreover, was no longer the possession of a privileged class, of clergy and *ministeriales*, but was a necessity for any merchant and many craftsmen. Its purpose was utilitarian and didactic. The merchant saw the world he lived in as important in itself, for in this world lay his goods and his markets. Facts concerning the world, therefore, became valuable *per se*. The stress on facts or that which is conceived of as factual, the emphasis on *matter*, whether of fictional narrative or non-fictional exposition, is an expression of the post-chivalric view of the world. The increase of purely secular studies —medicine, law—at the universities and schools reinforced this predilection for the factual, which is also reflected in the development of nominalism in the fourteenth century. The fact, that which is conceived of as constituting 'reality', is most clearly imparted in prose.[3] True, the fourteenth and fifteenth centuries saw the emergence of such genres as the love allegories in late Middle High German, and to some extent the tradition of the courtly love lyric continued in favour. But both of these superficially courtly genres exhibit a high degree of realism and testify mainly to an awareness of the courtly tradition as an aristocratic phenomenon. The courtly love lyric of the chivalric period was as much a thing of the past as chivalric civilization. It now became an object of the collector and compiler. Most of the famous collections transmitting the classical Middle High German lyric—the Manesse or large Heidelberg MS., the small Heidelberg MS., the Weingartner and Jenaer MSS.—date from this period. In short, the merchant read, and perhaps even wrote, poetry with courtly trappings much in the same spirit in which he bought land and a title. He expressed his principal interests, however, in his predilection for the realistic, didactic, or plainly narrative presentation of fact or pseudo-fact. Elsewhere in western and southern Europe these interests in the temporal, the mundane, together with a veneration for ancient Greek and Roman culture, formed one of many preludes to the Renaissance. Whereas Germany shared, to some degree, in the currents of Humanistic thought, this combination of interests led not to a Renaissance, but to the essentially middle-class Reformation, nourished by nationalistic sentiment.

The social and economic disruptions which characterized the Interregnum contributed to an acceleration of the trend toward urbanization by making it necessary for the cities and their merchants to take effective measures for their protection. Feudal German society emerged from the Interregnum and the period immediately following it, prepared to become a predominantly middle-class society. True, in terms of political power, Germany's Age of the Princes had dawned, ushered in above all by the seven electors; but the princes came to depend increasingly on the backing provided by trade and an urban middle class.

With the accession of Rudolf of Habsburg, the empire, despite its pretensions, had shrunk to no more than the confines of central Europe. Its Italian and Sicilian adventures had closed with the death of the last Hohenstaufen. For another five hundred years the Holy Roman Empire tottered along, but, in the words of Voltaire, it was neither holy, nor Roman, nor an empire.

Genealogical Tables

THE CAROLINGIAN DYNASTY

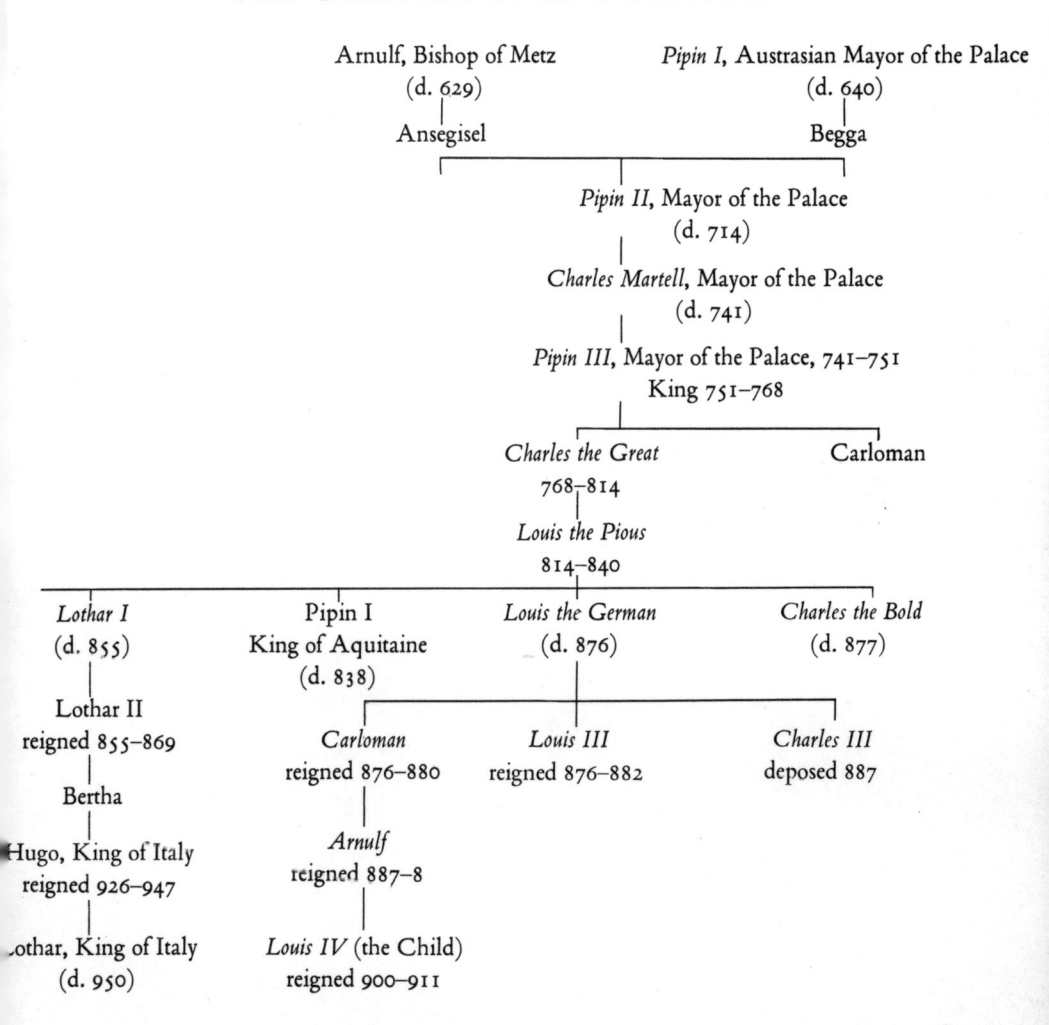

Arnulf, Bishop of Metz (d. 629) — Ansegisel

Pipin I, Austrasian Mayor of the Palace (d. 640) — Begga

Pipin II, Mayor of the Palace (d. 714)

Charles Martell, Mayor of the Palace (d. 741)

Pipin III, Mayor of the Palace, 741–751; King 751–768

- Charles the Great 768–814
  - Louis the Pious 814–840
    - Lothar I (d. 855)
      - Lothar II reigned 855–869
        - Bertha
          - Hugo, King of Italy reigned 926–947
            - Lothar, King of Italy (d. 950)
    - Pipin I, King of Aquitaine (d. 838)
      - Carloman reigned 876–880
        - Arnulf reigned 887–8
          - Louis IV (the Child) reigned 900–911
    - Louis the German (d. 876)
      - Louis III reigned 876–882
    - Charles the Bold (d. 877)
      - Charles III deposed 887
- Carloman

165

Medieval Civilization in Germany

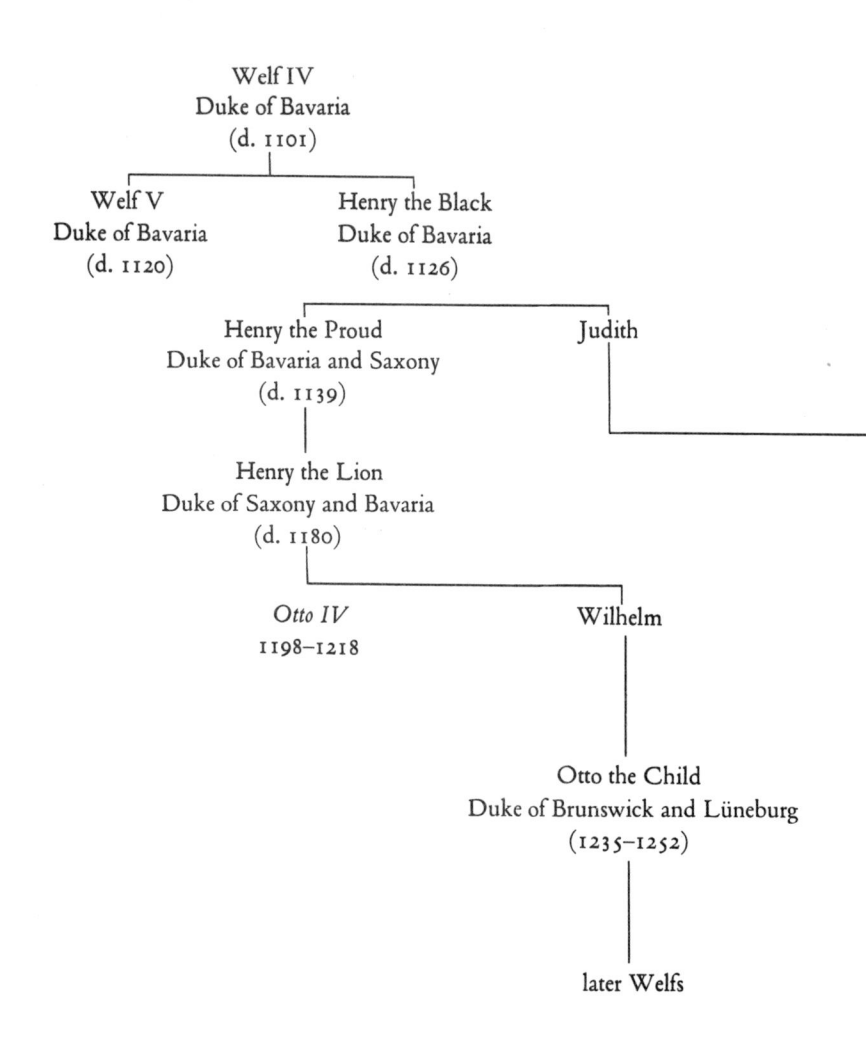

THE HOHENSTAUFEN AND WELF DYNASTIES

WELFS

Welf IV
Duke of Bavaria
(d. 1101)
├── Welf V
│   Duke of Bavaria
│   (d. 1120)
└── Henry the Black
    Duke of Bavaria
    (d. 1126)
    ├── Henry the Proud
    │   Duke of Bavaria and Saxony
    │   (d. 1139)
    │   │
    │   Henry the Lion
    │   Duke of Saxony and Bavaria
    │   (d. 1180)
    │   ├── Otto IV
    │   │   1198–1218
    │   └── Wilhelm
    │   │
    │   Otto the Child
    │   Duke of Brunswick and Lüneburg
    │   (1235–1252)
    │   │
    │   later Welfs
    └── Judith

Genealogical Tables

HOHENSTAUFEN

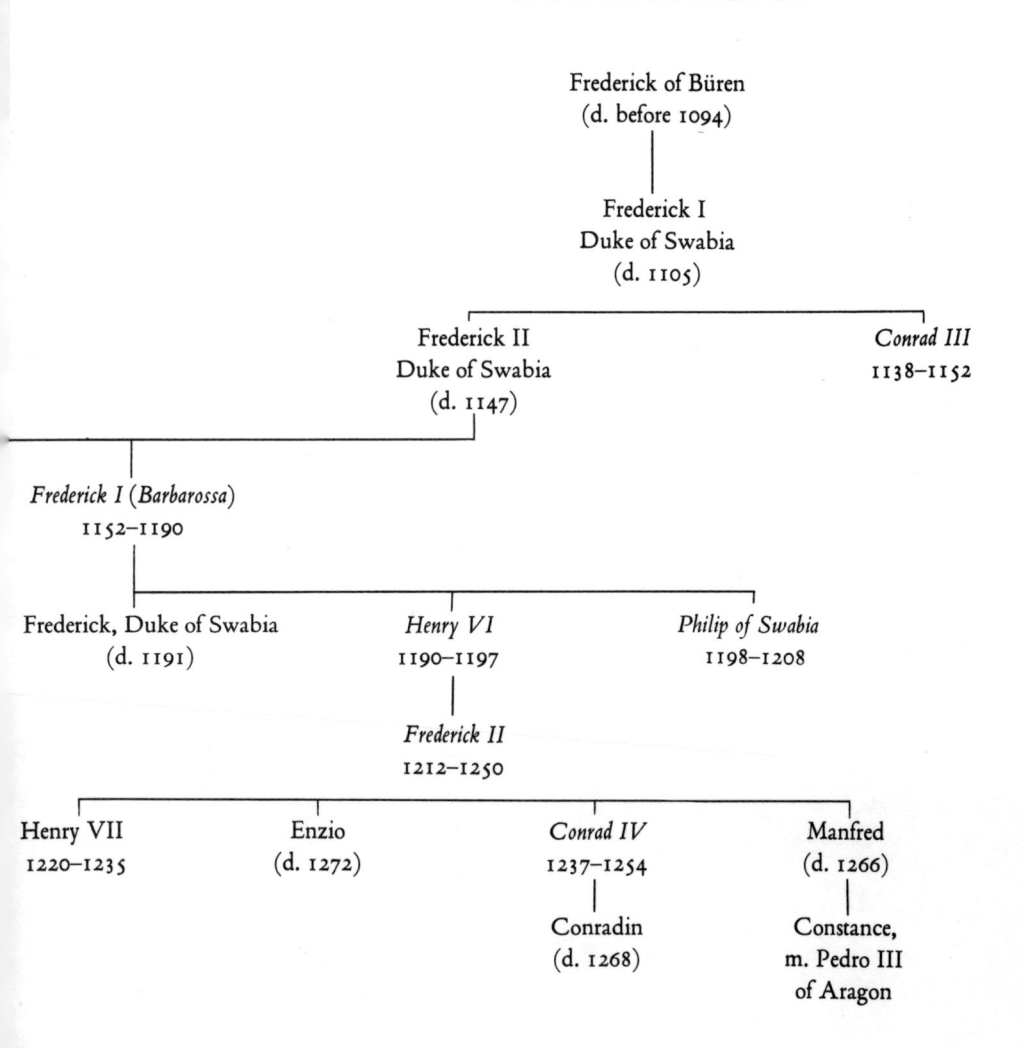

Frederick of Büren
(d. before 1094)

Frederick I
Duke of Swabia
(d. 1105)

Frederick II Duke of Swabia (d. 1147) — Conrad III 1138–1152

Frederick I (Barbarossa) 1152–1190

Frederick, Duke of Swabia (d. 1191) — *Henry VI* 1190–1197 — *Philip of Swabia* 1198–1208

Frederick II 1212–1250

Henry VII 1220–1235 — Enzio (d. 1272) — *Conrad IV* 1237–1254 — Manfred (d. 1266)

Conradin (d. 1268)

Constance, m. Pedro III of Aragon

167

THE SAXON AND SALIAN DYNASTIES

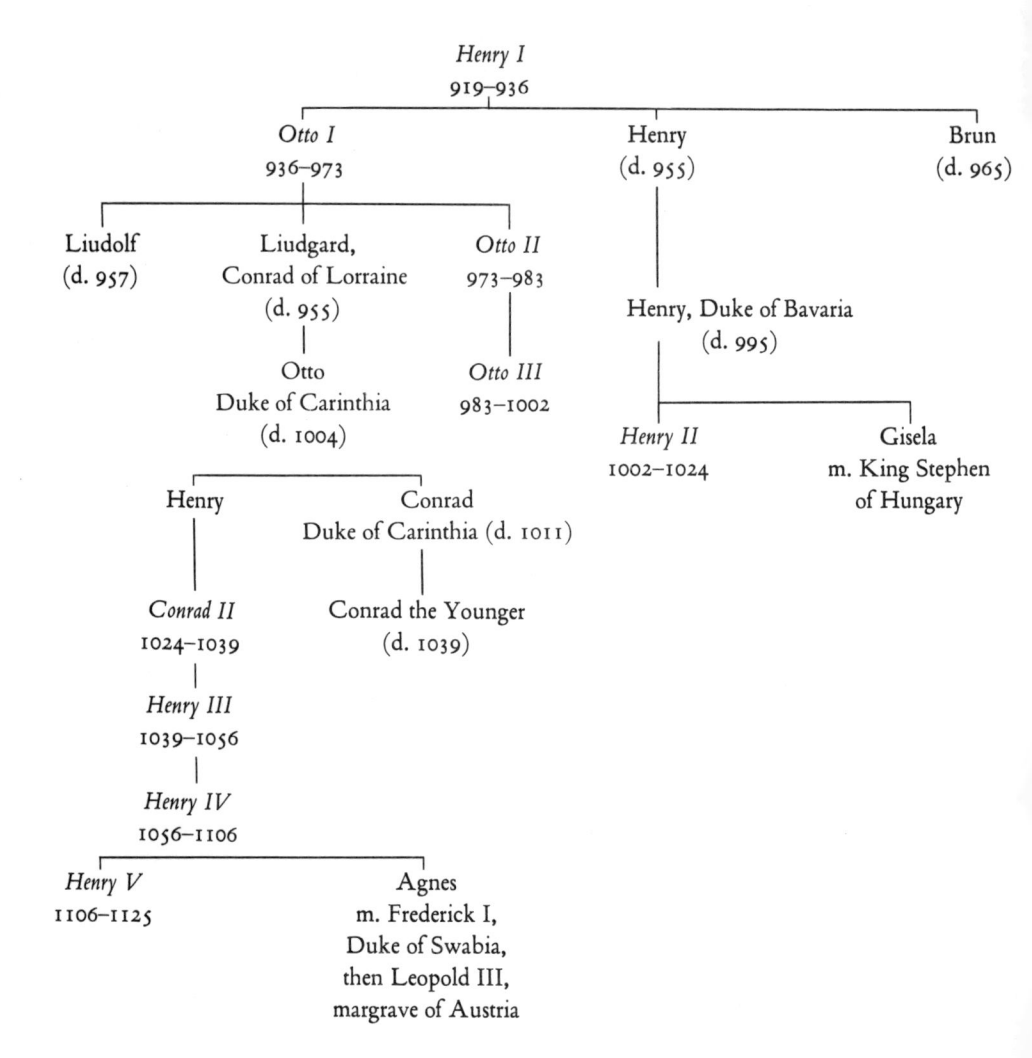

Henry I
919–936

Otto I — Henry — Brun
936–973 — (d. 955) — (d. 965)

Liudolf — Liudgard, — *Otto II*
(d. 957) — Conrad of Lorraine — 973–983
— (d. 955)

Otto — *Otto III*
Duke of Carinthia — 983–1002
(d. 1004)

Henry, Duke of Bavaria
(d. 995)

Henry II — Gisela
1002–1024 — m. King Stephen
— of Hungary

Henry — Conrad
— Duke of Carinthia (d. 1011)

Conrad II — Conrad the Younger
1024–1039 — (d. 1039)

Henry III
1039–1056

Henry IV
1056–1106

Henry V — Agnes
1106–1125 — m. Frederick I,
— Duke of Swabia,
— then Leopold III,
— margrave of Austria

168

Notes on the Text

CHAPTER I

1 It must be recalled, in this respect, that the viewpoint of nineteenth-century and modern historiography from which the concepts *sacrum imperium* and *sacerdotum* are regarded as two poles around which political and intellectual activity can be clustered, is conditioned by later medieval and post-medieval thought patterns. Cf. Friedrich Heer, *Aufgang Europas* (Vienna, Zurich, 1949), pp. 9–12.

2 In literary histories the *Evangelienbuch* of Otfrid is often referred to as a gospel harmony. This is a misnomer. Otfrid makes no attempt to 'harmonize' the disparities of the Gospels after the model, for instance, of Tatian's *Diatessaron*. He merely uses now this, now that Gospel as a basis for his narrative.

3 The classical definition of gradualism has been given by Günther Müller, in *Deutsche Vierteljahrsschrift* II (1924), 681–720. Gradualistic thought, however, cannot be regarded as 'typical' for the Middle Ages to the degree which Müller claims for it.

4 The most concise presentation of medieval aesthetics, stressing neo-platonic influences, is to be found in Rosario Assunto, *Die Theorie des Schönen im Mittelalter* (Cologne, 1963).

5 This is basically the classic theory of the origin of feudalism as advanced by Heinrich Brunner, 'Der Reiterdienst und die Anfänge des Lehnwesens,' *Zeitschrift der Savigny-Stiftung für Rechtsgeschichte*, Germ. Abt. VIII (1887), 1–38. A lucid summary of this as well as conflicting theories is to be found in Lynn White, Jr., *Medieval Technology and Social Change* (Oxford, 1964), 2–14. Professor White presents the first full investigation of the role of the stirrup in this context; *ibid.* pp. 14–38.

6 Cf. Assunto, p. 79. For the Carolingian reaction to the iconoclastic controversy, cf. Gert Haendler, *Die Epochen karolingischer Theologie* (Berlin, 1958).

7 For the development of Carolingian from late Roman and early Christian art, as well as an examination of the varying role of space and its implications, cf. Roger Hinks, *Carolingian Art* (Ann Arbor, 1962).

8 The plan (c. 820) of the monastery of St Gallen mentions goldsmiths, ironsmiths, shieldmakers, armourers, carpenters, fullers, tanners, cobblers, and saddlers.

CHAPTER II

1 The most lucid interpretation of political developments in the Ottonian, Salian, and Hohenstaufen periods is that of Geoffrey Barraclough, *The Origins of Modern Germany* (New York, 1947). I am greatly indebted to Professor Barraclough's work in my presentation of the political history of these periods.
2 An excellent survey of economic conditions during this and succeeding periods, with a critical use of available statistics and estimates, is provided by Heinrich Bechtel, *Wirtschafts- und Sozialgeschichte Deutschlands* (Munich, 1967).
3 For the text of the original cf. *Das Register Gregors VII*, ed. E. Caspar, *Monumenta Historiae Germanica* (Berlin. 1920), pp. 202–208, 270–271, 312–314.
4 For the original text, cf. *Die Briefe Heinrichs IV*, ed. C. Erdmann *Deutsches Mittelalter. Kritische Studientexte des Reichsinstituts für ältere deutsche Geschichtskunde (Monumenta Germaniae Historica)* I (Leipzig, 1937), No. 12, pp. 15–17. The transmission of the text, however, is literary rather than archival: it is included in Bruno's *De bello Saxonico* (c. 67), as well as in the Codex Udalrici, an exemplary collection of poems and letters compiled in 1125, and in the St Emmeram collection Clm 14096.
5 I have added the last phrase as transmitted in the Codex Udalrici: 'per secula dampnande.'
6 For a general survey of this period with some stress on currents of contemporary public opinion, cf. Frederick Hertz, *The Development of the German Public Mind* (New York, 1957), p. 100–101.
7 A detailed analysis of these currents, particularly of the 'Bavarian School' is presented by E. F. Bange, *Eine bayerische Malerschule des XI. und XII. Jahrhunderts* (Munich, 1923).
8 Notker Balbulus is frequently referred to as the originator of the sequence in German literary histories. It is, however, quite likely that the sequence was known before Notker.

Notes on the Text

9 The view of cluniac influences on German literature which is commonly presented in German literary histories sorely needs revision. For a vigorous criticism of the views of some germanists, cf. Friedrich Heer, *Aufgang Europas* (Vienna, Zurich, 1949), pp. 12-13.

CHAPTER III

1 Ottonis Episcopi Frisingensis et Rahewini *Gesta Friderici* (Berlin, 1965) III, 12-13.
2 *Ibid.*, II, 32.
3 It must be recalled that medieval philosophical realism has nothing to do with 'realism' in the literary sense. The philosophical realist ascribes 'reality' to universals, the nominalist regards universals merely as 'nomina,' and views only individuals as 'real.'
4 The role of light—not as source of brilliance, but of gentle suffusion—and of a basic geometric form in Gothic architecture is discussed by Otto von Simson, *Die gotische Kathedrale* (Darmstadt, 1968), pp. 36-68.
5 Erwin Panofsky's analyses of the solution of technical architectural problems posed by contradictory possibilities shed valuable light on the intellectual relationship between Gothic architecture and scholastic philosophy; cf. his *Gothic Architecture and Scholasticism* (Cleveland and New York, 1961).
6 Etienne Gilson, *History of Christian Philosophy in the Middle Ages* (New York, 1955), pp. 293-294. The passage is a quotation from M. Grabmann, *Geschichte der scholastischen Methode* (Berlin, 1956). Both works are fundamental for any orientation in medieval scholasticism.
7 The effects of the increased complexity of political affairs are discussed by R. W. Southern, *The Making of the Middle Ages* (New Haven and London, 1962), pp. 80 ff.
8 For an analysis of the process of oral composition and transmission of long epic poems cf. Albert B. Lord, *The Singer of Tales* (Cambridge, Mass., 1960); Franz H. Bäuml and Donald J. Ward, 'Zur mündlichen Überlieferung des Nibelungenliedes,' *Deutsche Vierteljahrsschrift*, XLI (1967), 351-390 and Franz H. Bäuml, 'Der Übergang mündlicher zur Artes-bestimmten Literatur des Mittelalters: Gedanken und Bedenken' *Fachliteratur des Mittelalters. Festschrift Gerhard Eis* (Stuttgart, 1968), pp. 1-10 contain biographical data to the relevant literature.

9 For a thorough analysis of this poem cf. Peter Wapnewski, 'Des Kürenberger's Falkenlied,' *Euphorion,* LIII (1959), 1–19. It is curious that, on the basis of a correct interpretation of all pertinent evidence, Wapnewski should regard the poem as a plaint—a conclusion which, in my opinion, is untenable in the light of the evidence adduced.

10 This identification, however, uses the term 'Gothic' in a sense different from that given it by some German literary historians who, in applying it to poets like Conrad of Würzburg, seem to regard it merely as denoting a style typified by a great number of components.

11 For a discussion and criticism of the allegorical interpretation of secular medieval literature cf. Jean Misrahi, 'Symbolism and Allegory in Arthurian Romance,' *Romance Philology,* XVII (1964), 555–569.

12 It is a common mistake of literary critics, arising from their traditional preoccupation with the creative act at the expense of the perceptive act, to assume that each period or each culture or cultural epoch exhibits, or is characterized by only one form of perception, such as the allegorical, the symbolic, or the realistic mode. In fact, however, any number of perceptual modes coexist under the dominance of one. Just as it is possible for the 'realistic' three-dimensional mode of perception to be augmented by the symbolic mode, so the symbolic mode of perception, which dominated much of medieval culture, was accompanied by the 'realistic' mode. The medieval perceiver could receive aesthetic stimuli as 'realistic' or 'illusionistic' as well as symbolic, in much the same way as the modern perceiver can receive both modes. The determinant lies partly in the work of art, partly in the critical sophistication, the aesthetic awareness of the perceiver, and partly in his cultural environment. That the same work of art could be perceived in the symbolic as well as in the 'illusionistic' mode is evident, for instance, in the view of the *Nibelungenlied* which must be posited for the courtly reader at the time of its composition (cf. p. 141), and that expressed by the plaint, *Die Klage,* written not long afterwards. A number of recent psychological studies have demonstrated that, cross-culturally, aesthetic awareness is a relatively stable factor, i.e. a factor at least partially independent of the cultural environment. It follows that the same stability of aesthetic awareness as a criterion of perception can be assumed to be operative diachronically. Cf. C. C. Pratt, 'The Stability of Aesthetic Judgments', *Journal of Aesthetics and Art Criticism,* XV (1956), 1–11; I. L. Child

and L. Siroto, 'Bakwele and American Esthetic Evaluations Compared', *Ethnology*, IV (1965), 349–360; S. Iwao and I. L. Child, 'Comparison of Esthetic Judgments by American Experts and by Japanese Potters', *Journal of Social Psychology*, LXVIII (1966), 27–33. R. W. Skager, C. B. Schultz, S. P. Klein, 'Points of View about Preference as Tools in the Analysis of Creative Products', *Perceptual and Motor Skills*, XXII (1966), 83–94; C. S. Ford, E. T. Prothro, I. L. Child, 'Some Transcultural Comparisons of Esthetic Judgment', *Journal of Social Psychology*, LXVIII (1966), 19–26; I. L. Child, 'The Experts and the Bridge of Judgment that Crosses Every Cultural Gap', *Psychology Today*, II (1968), 25–29.

13 The interpretation of Kriemhild's function offered here differs from the traditional view of her 'characterization' as a sweet young thing transmogrified by events into an avenging fury. This generally accepted view is tenable only if the text is adapted to one's preconceptions. Kriemhild's famous falcon-dream and her subsequent conversation with her mother (st. 13–17), which serve as basis for this tradition, yield an entirely different meaning to the careful reader. Kriemhild dreams that she trained a falcon, and that two eagles killed it. Her mother tells her that the falcon signifies a man, whom she will soon lose if God does not protect him. Kriemhild answers that she wants to have nothing to do with love, and that she wants to remain as beautiful as she is, so that [st. 15, 4: daz] she will never suffer distress on account of the love of a man. The usual reluctance on the part of editors to come to terms with the word 'daz' in st. 15, 4 is understandable: a recognition of the precise syntactic function of the word would result in the destruction of the cherished image of a naive young Kriemhild. The combination of the two wishes—to remain attractive and to avoid possible distress resulting from love—is a clear expression of a desire for dominance: Kriemhild's lasting beauty will ensure her domination of men from whom she will remain aloof. The word 'daz,' i.e. 'so that', makes Kriemhild's statement even more pointed: she wants to remain as beautiful as she is, in order to maintain permanently the dominance over men which beauty gives her, and simultaneously she views this dominance as a means for remaining emotionally aloof. The word 'daz' is part of the syntactical system of the sentence and can be interpreted in no other way. Kriemhild's words and actions elsewhere bear out this interpretation. Cf. Arnold H. Price,

'Characterization in the Nibelungenlied', *Monatshefte,* LI (1959), 341–350.

14 The traditional view of Hagen as a cowardly murderer is, of course, untenable. Hagen drives the spear into Siegfried's back while the latter is drinking from a well solely because he knows that this is Siegfried's only vulnerable spot.

15 For the ambivalent actions of Dietrich, cf. Hans Kuhn in the *Anzeiger für deutsches Altertum,* LXXVI (1965), 9–14.

CHAPTER IV

1 The *Tagelied* or *aubade* is a subgenre of the courtly love lyric. Its theme is the necessity of the lovers' parting at the break of day.

2 A concise introduction to the works of these mystics is provided by J. M. Clark, *The Great German Mystics: Eckhart, Tauler and Suso* (Oxford, 1949).

3 On the increase in the use of prose as well as late medieval literary developments in general, cf. H. J. Chaytor, *From Script to Print* (Cambridge, 1950), pp. 83 ff.

Bibliography

PRIMARY SOURCES

BARBER, C. C. *An Old High German Reader.* Oxford, 1964.
BARTSCH, K. *Deutsche Liederdichter des zwölften bis vierzehnten Jahrhunderts.* Berlin, 1928.
BEENKEN, H. *Romanische Skulptur in Deutschland.* Leipzig, 1924.
BELL, C. H., transl., *Peasant Life in Old German Epics: Meier Helmbrecht, Der arme Heinrich.* New York, 1931.
BOECKLER, A. *Abendländische Miniaturen.* Berlin/Leipzig, 1930.
— *Deutsche Buchmalerei Vorgotischer Zeit.* Königstein im Taunus, 1959.
BOSAU, HELMOLD V. *Slawenchronik,* tr. H. Stoob (Ausg. Quellen zur deutschen Geschichte des Mittelalters, Freiherr vom Stein Gedächtnisausg.). Darmstadt, 1963.
BRAUNE, W. *Old High German Grammar.* San Francisco, 1955.
Brunonis Saxonicum Bellum (Ausg. Quellen zur dt. Gesch. d. Mittelalters, Frhr. vom Stein Gedächtnisausg. XII). Berlin, 1963.
DE BOOR, H., ed. *Mittelalter. Texte und Zeugnisse* (Die deutsche Literatur). Munich, 1965.
Echternach, The Golden Gospels of. ed. Metz. London, 1957.
Einhardi Vita Caroli Magni (Ausg. Quellen zur dt. Gesch. d. Mittelalters, Frhr. vom Stein Gedächtnisausg., V). Berlin, 1955.
GOLDSCHMIDT, A. *German Illumination.* 2 vols. Florence, 1928.
GOTTFRIED V. STRASSBURG, *Tristan,* ed. Ranke. Berlin/Frankfurt, 1949. *Tristan,* tr. Hatto. Harmondsworth and Baltimore, 1960.
HARTMANN V. AUE, *Erec,* ed. Leitzmann. Tübingen, 1957.
— *Gregorius,* ed. Neumann. Wiesbaden, 1958.
— *Gregorius, the Good Sinner.* New York, 1966.
— *Der arme Heinrich,* ed. Paul and Wolff. Tübingen, 1953.
— *Iwein,* ed. Lachmann and Wolff. Berlin, 1959.
KRAUS, CARL V., ed. *Deutsche Gedichte des zwölften Jahrhunderts.* 2 vols. Halle, 1894.
— *Deutsche Liederdichter des 13. Jahrhunderts.* Tübingen, 1958.

Kudrun, ed. Stackmann. Wiesbaden, 1966.
LAMPERT VON HERSFELD, *Annalen* (Ausg. Quellen zur dt. Gesch. d. Mittelalters, Frhr. vom Stein Gedächtnisausg., XIII). Berlin, 1957.
LANGOSCH, K., ed. and transl. *Hymnen und Vagantenlieder. Lateinische Lyrik des Mittelalters.* Darmstadt, 1958.
— *Geistliche Spiele. Lateinische Dramen des Mittelalters.* Darmstadt, 1961.
— *Waltharius, Ruodlieb, Märchenepen. Lateinische Epik des Mittelalters.* Darmstadt, 1967.
VON DER LEYEN, F., ed. *Deutsche Dichtung des Mittelalters.* Frankfurt, 1962.
Minnesangs Frühling, ed. Lachmann, v. Kraus. Leipzig, 1959.
Nibelungenlied, ed. Bartsch, De Boor. Wiesbaden, 1959, transl. A. T. Hatto. Harmondsworth, 1965.
OTTO BISCHOF VON FREISING, *Chronik* (Ausg. Quellen zur dt. Gesch. d. Mittelalters, Frhr. vom Stein Gedächtnisausg.). Berlin, 1960.
— *Two Cities: A Chronicle of Universal History of the Year 1146 AD,* ed. Mierow. New York, 1966.
OTTO BISCHOF VON FREISING, and RAHEWIN. *Die Taten Friedrichs* (Ausg. Quellen zur dt. Gesch. d. Mittelalters, Frhr. vom Stein Gedächtnisausg). Berlin, 1965.
PINDER, W. *Deutsche Dome des Mittelalters.* Königstein im Taunus, 1960.
REITZENSTEIN, A. FRHR. V. *Deutsche Plastik der Früh- und Hochgotik.* Königstein im Taunus, 1962.
STANGE, A. *Deutsche Gotische Malerei.* Königstein im Taunus, 1964.
Thietmari Merseburgensis episcopi chronicon (Ausg. Quellen zur dt. Gesch. d. Mittelalters, Frhr. vom Stein Gedächtnisausg.). Berlin, 1957.
WALTHER VON DER VOGELWEIDE, *Lieder,* ed. Maurer. Tübingen, 1960, 1962.
Widukindi monachi Corbeiensis rerum gestarum Saxonicarum libri tres, ed. Hirsch. Hanover, 1935.
Wiponis gesta Chuonradi II imperatoris (Ausg. Quellen zur dt. Gesch. d. Mittelalters, Frhr. vom Stein Gedächtnisausg.). Berlin, 1961.
WOLFRAM VON ESCHENBACH, *Parzival, Lieder, Titurel,* ed. Hartl. Berlin, 1952.
— *Parzival,* tr. Mustard and Passage. New York, 1961.

Bibliography

SECONDARY LITERATURE
(For current publications in the relevant fields, consult Richard H. Rouse, *Serial Bibliographies for Medieval Studies*. Berkeley/Los Angeles, 1969.)

AINAUD, J. AND HELD, A. *Romanesque Painting*. New York, 1963.
ALBERT, J. J. *Die Musikanschauung des Mittelalters und ihre Grundlagen*. Leipzig, 1905.
ASSUNTO, R. *Die Theorie des Schönen im Mittelalter,* Cologne, 1963.
AUERBACH, E. *Mimesis*. New York, 1957.
Ausstellung Romanische Kunst in Österreich. Krems, 1964.
BAETKE, W. *Die Aufnahme des Christentums durch die Germanen*. Darmstadt, 1968.
BANDMANN, G. *Mittelalterliche Architektur als Bedeutungsträger*. Berlin, 1951.
BANGE, E. F. *Eine bayrische Malerschule des XI und XII Jahrhunderts*. Munich, 1923.
BARRACLOUGH, G. *The Origins of Modern Germany*. New York, 1963.
— *Medieval Germany 911–1250*, 2 vols. New York, 1968.
BECHTEL, H. *Wirtschafts- und Sozialgeschichte Deutschlands*. Munich, 1967.
BELOW, G. V. *Das ältere deutsche Städtewesen und Bürgertum*. Bielefeld/Leipzig, 1925.
BEUMANN, H. *Heidenmission und Kreuzzugsgedanke in der deutschen Ostpolitik des Mittelalters*. Darmstadt, 1963.
— *Ideengeschichtliche Studien zu Einhard und anderen Geschichtsschreibern des frühen Mittelalters*. Darmstadt, 1962.
BLOCH, M. *Feudal Society*, 2 vols. Chicago, 1964.
BOOZ, P. *Der Baumeister der Gotik*. Munich/Berlin, 1956.
BOSL, K. *Die Reichsministerialität der Salier und Staufer*. Stuttgart, 1950/51.
BOSTOCK, J. K. *A Handbook on Old High German Literature*. Oxford, 1955.
BRACKMANN, A. *Zur politischen Bedeutung der kluniazensischen Bewegung*. Darmstadt, 1958.
BRINKMANN, H. *Zu Wesen und Form mittelalterlicher Dichtung*. Halle, 1928.
BRUYNE, E. DE *Aesthetics of the Middle Ages*. New York, 1950.

BRYCE, J. *The Holy Roman Empire*. New York, 1961.
BÜHLER, J. *Die Kultur des Mittelalters*. Stuttgart, 1954.
BURGER, H. O. *Annalen der deutschen Literatur*. Stuttgart, 1952/53.
Cambridge Medieval History, Vols. III and V. Cambridge, 1957.
CARLYLE, SIR R. W. AND CARLYLE, A. J. *History of Medieval Political Theory in the West*. Edinburgh, 1903/28, New York, 1936.
CLARK, J. M. *The Great German Mystics: Eckhart, Tauler, Suso*. Oxford, 1949.
CROMBIE, A. C. *Medieval and Early Modern Science*, 2 vols. New York, 1959.
CURTIUS, E. R. *Europäische Literatur und Lateinisches Mittelalter*. Bern, 1954.
DAENELL, E. *Die Blütezeit der deutschen Hanse*. Berlin, 1905/6.
DEANESLY, M. *A History of the Medieval Church 590–1500*. London, 1959.
DE BOOR, H. AND NEWALD, R. *Geschichte der deutschen Literatur*, Vols. I-III. Munich, 1964.
DEHIO, G. *Geschichte der deutschen Kunst*, Vols. I-III. Berlin/Leipzig, 1921/26.
DEMPF, A. *Sacrum Imperium. Geschichts- und Staatsphilosophie des Mittelalters und der politischen Renaissance*. Darmstadt, 1954.
DOPSCH, A. *Die Wirtschaftsentwicklung der Karolingerzeit vornehmlich in Deutschland*. Weimar, 1921/22.
DÜMMLER, E. *Geschichte des ostfränkischen Reichs*. Darmstadt, 1968.
DUNGERN, O. FRHR. V. *Adelsherrschaft im Mittelalter*. Munich, 1927.
— *Thronfolgerecht und Blutsverwandtschaft der deutschen Kaiser seit Karl dem Grossen*. Berlin, 1910.
DUNNING, W. A. *History of Political Theories, Ancient and Medieval*. New York, 1902.
DVORÁK, M. *Idealismus und Naturalismus in der gotischen Skulptur und Malerei*. Vienna, 1918.
EASTON, S. C. AND WIERUSZOWSKI, H. *The Era of Charlemagne: Frankish State and Society*. New York, 1961.
EHRISMANN, G. *Geschichte der deutschen Literatur bis zum Ausgang des Mittelalters*, 4 vols. Munich, 1922/35.
ERDMANN, C. *Die Entstehung des Kreuzzugsgedankens*. Darmstadt, 1968.

Bibliography

GALL, E. *Die gotische Baukunst in Frankreich und Deutschland.* Leipzig, 1925.
— *Cathedrals and Abbey Churches of the Rhine.* London, 1962, New York, n.d.
GANSHOF, F. L. *Feudalism.* New York, 1961.
GILSON, E. *History of Christian Philosophy in the Middle Ages.* New York, 1955.
GLUNZ, H. *Literaturästhetik des europäischen Mittelalters.* Bochum, 1937.
GRABMANN, M. *Geschichte der scholastischen Methode*, 2 vols. Freiburg im Br., 1909/11.
GRUNDMANN, H. *Religiöse Bewegungen im Mittelalter.* Darmstadt, 1961.
HÄPKE, R. *Wirtschaftsgeschichte*, I, *Mittelalter und Merkantilismus.* Leipzig, 1928.
HALLER, J. *Von den Karolingern zu den Staufern. Die altdeutsche Kaiserzeit (900–1250).* Berlin, 1942.
HALLINGER, K. *Gorze-Kluny. Studien zu den monastischen Lebensformen und Gegensätzen im Hochmittelalter* in *Studia Anselmiana,* Vols. XXII, XXIII. 1950/51.
HAMPE, K. *Deutsche Kaisergeschichte in der Zeit der Salier und Staufer.* Leipzig, 1922.
— *Das Hochmittelalter. Geschichte des Abendlandes von 900 bis 1250.* Berlin, 1932.
— *Herrschergestalten des deutschen Mittelalters.* Leipzig, 1939.
HASHAGEN, J. 'Über die ideengeschichtliche Stellung des staufischen Zeitalters', *Deutsche Vierteljahrsschrift,* IX, 350–362. 1931.
HASKINS, C. H. *The Renaissance of the Twelfth Century.* Cambridge, Mass., 1927.
HAUCK, A. *Kirchengeschichte Deutschlands.* Berlin, 1952.
HAUSER, A. *The Social History of Art,* 2 vols. New York, 1957.
HAUTTMANN, M. 'Der Wandel der Bildvorstellungen in der deutschen Dichtung und Kunst des Romanischen Zeitalters', *Festschrift Heinrich Wölfflin,* 63–81. Munich, 1924.
HEMPEL, E. *Geschichte der deutschen Baukunst.* Munich, 1949.
HERTZ, F. *The Development of the German Public Mind.* New York, 1957.
HEUSLER, A. *Die altgermanische Dichtung.* Darmstadt, 1957.
HINKS, R. *Carolingian Art.* Ann Arbor, 1962.

Hirsch, H. *Das Recht der Königserhebung durch Kaiser und Papst in hohen Mittelalter.* Darmstadt, 1962.
Hofmeister, A. *Das Wormser Konkordat.* Darmstadt, 1962.
Holtzmann, R. *Geschichte der sächsischen Kaiserzeit.* Darmstadt, 1961.
Hotz, W. *Kleine Kunstgeschichte der deutschen Burg.* Darmstadt, 1965.
Huth, H. *Künstler und Werkstatt der Spätgotik.* Darmstadt, 1967.
Inama-Sternegg, K. Th. v. *Deutsche Wirtschaftsgeschichte,* 3 vols. Leipzig, 1879/1901.
Irtenkauf, W. *Hirsau. Geschichte und Kultur.* Lindau, 1959.
Jäger, O. *Geschichte des Mittelalters* (vol. II of *Weltgeschichte*). Bielefeld and Leipzig, 1903.
Jantzen, H. *Über den gotischen Kirchenraum.* Freiburg im Br., 1927.
— *Ottonische Kunst.* Munich, 1947.
— *Kunst der Gotik.* Hamburg, 1957.
Just, L. ed. *Deutsche Geschichte bis zum Ausgang des Mittelalters.* Frankfurt, 1957.
Kämpf, H. *Herrschaft und Staat im Mittelalter.* Darmstadt, 1956.
— *Die Entstehung des deutschen Reiches.* Darmstadt, 1956.
— *Canossa als Wende.* Darmstadt, 1963.
Knowles, D. *The Evolution of Medieval Thought.* New York, 1962.
Knüll, B. *Historische Geographie Deutschlands im Mittelalter.* Breslau, 1903.
Köpke, R. and Dümmler, E. *Kaiser Otto der Grosse.* Darmstadt, 1962.
Kötzschke, R. *Allgemeine Wirtschaftsgeschichte des Mittelalters.* Jena, 1924.
Kraus, F. X. *Geschichte der christlichen Kunst.* Freiburg i. Br., 1897.
Kuhn, H. 'Zur Deutung der künstlerischen Form des Mittelalters', *Studium Generale,* II, 114–120. 1949.
— 'Zum neuen Bild vom Mittelalter', *Deutsche Vierteljahrsschrift,* XXIV, 530–544. 1950.
— 'Soziale Realität und dichterische Fiktion am Beispiel der höfischen Ritterdichtung Deutschlands', *Soziologie und Leben,* ed. C. Brinkmann, pp. 195–219. Tübingen, 1952.
— 'Gestalten und Lebenskräfte der frühmittelhochdeutschen Dichtung', *Deutsche Vierteljahrsschrift,* XXVII, 1–30. 1953.

Bibliography

LAMMERS, W., ed. *Geschichtsdenken und Geschichtsbild im Mittelalter*. Darmstadt, 1961.
LANGOSCH, K. *Profil des lateinischen Mittelalters*. Darmstadt, 1965.
LE GOFF, J. *La Civilisation de l'Occident Médiéval*. Paris, 1965.
MANITIUS, M. *Geschichte der lateinischen Literatur des Mittelalters*, 3 vols. Munich, 1911/23.
MAYER, TH., ed. *Adel und Bauern im deutschen Staat des Mittelalters*. Leipzig, 1943.
MIDDLETON, J. H. *Illuminated Manuscripts in Classical and Medieval Times*. Cambridge, 1892.
MITTEIS, H. *Der Staat des hohen Mittelalters*. Weimar, 1944.
MOSER, H. 'Dichtung und Wirklichkeit im Hochmittelalter', *Wirkendes Wort*, V, 79–91. 1954/55.
MOWATT, D. J. AND SACKER, H. *The Nibelungenlied*. Toronto, 1967.
MÜHLBACHER, E. *Deutsche Geschichte unter den Karolingern*. Darmstadt, 1959.
MÜLLER, G. 'Gradualismus', *Deutsche Vierteljahrsschrift*, II, 681–720. 1924.
NADLER, J. *Literaturgeschichte der deutschen Stämme und Landschaften*. Regensburg, 1912. (for the illustrations)
NAUMANN, H. 'Literaturbericht zur höfischen Epik', *Deutsche Vierteljahrsschrift*, XXI, Referatenheft, 1 ff. 1943.
NORMAN, F. 'Hildebrand and Hadubrand', *German Life and Letters*, II, 325–34. 1957/58.
OMAN, SIR C. W. C. *History of the Art of War in the Middle Ages*. London and Boston, 1924.
PFISTER, K. *Mittelalterliche Buchmalerei des Abendlandes*. Munich, 1922.
PINDER, W. *Die Kunst der deutschen Kaiserzeit bis zum Ende der staufischen Klassik*. Leipzig, 1937. Illustrations 1943.
PIRENNE, H. *Medieval Cities, Their Origins and the Revival of Trade*. Princeton, 1925.
RASHDALL, H. *Universities of Europe in the Middle Ages*. Oxford, 1895: repr. New York, 1963.
RASSOW, P. *Honor Imperii*. Darmstadt, 1961.
REITZENSTEIN, A. FRHR. V. *Deutsche Baukunst*. Stuttgart, 1956.

RUPP, H. 'Über das Verhältnis von deutscher und lateinischer Dichtung im 9.-12. Jahrhundert', *Germanisch-Romanische Monatsschrift*, XXXIX, 19-34. 1958.
SACKER, H. 'An Interpretation of Hartmann's *Iwein*', *Germanic Review*, XXXVI, 5-26. 1961.
—, *An Introduction to Wolfram's Parzival*. Cambridge, 1963.
SACKUR, E. *Die Cluniazenser in ihrer kirchlichen und allgemeingeschichtlichen Wirksamkeit bis zur Mitte des 11. Jahrhunderts.* Tübingen, 2 vols. 1892/94.
SALMON, P. *Literature in Medieval Germany*. London, 1967, New York, 1968.
SANDER, P. *Geschichte des deutschen Städtewesens*. Bonn/Leipzig, 1922.
SAUER, J. *Symbolik des Kirchengebäudes*. Freiburg im Br., 1902.
SCHACHNER, N. *The Medieval Universities*. New York, 1962.
SCHÄFER, D. *Die deutsche Hanse*. Bielefeld, 1914.
SCHERR, J. *Deutsche Kultur- und Sittengeschichte*. Wiesbaden, n.d.
SCHLOSSER, J. v. *Die Kunst des Mittelalters*. Vienna, 1923.
SCHLOSSER, J. AND KURZ, O. *Die Kunstliteratur*. Vienna, 1924.
SCHMEIDLER, B. *Das spätere Mittelalter von der Mitte des 13. Jahrhunderts bis zur Reformation*. Darmstadt, 1962.
SCHNEIDER, F. *Mittelalter bis zur Mitte des 13. Jahrhunderts*. Darmstadt, 1963.
SCHNEIDER, H. *Heldendichtung, Geistlichendichtung, Ritterdichtung*. Heidelberg, 1943.
SCHRÖDER, W. J. 'Das Nibelungenlied', *Beiträge zur Geschichte der deutschen Sprache und Literatur*, LXXVI, 56-143, Halle, 1954.
SCHULTZ, A. *Das höfische Leben zur Zeit der Minnesinger*, 2 vols. Leipzig, 1889; repr. New York, 1968.
SCHULZE, E. O. *Die Kolonisierung und Germanisierung der Gebiete zwischen Saale und Elbe*. Leipzig, 1896.
SCHWIETERING, J. *Die deutsche Dichtung des Mittelalters*. Darmstadt, 1957.
STAMMLER, W. AND LANGOSCH, K., eds. *Die deutsche Literatur des Mittelalters. Verfasserlexikon*. Berlin, 5 vols, 1933/55.
STEINEN, W. v. d. *Canossa*. Darmstadt, 1957.
SULLIVAN, R. E., ed. *The Coronation of Charlemagne. What did it signify?* Boston, 1959.

TAEUBER, W. *Geld und Kredit im Mittelalter*. Berlin, 1933.
TALBOT, C. H., ed. *The Anglo-Saxon Missionaries in Germany*. New York, 1954.
TAYLOR, H. O. *The Medieval Mind*, 2 vols. London, 1925.
TELLENBACH, G. *Church, State, and Christian Society at the Time of the Investiture Conquest*. New York, 1959.
THOMPSON, J. W. *East German Colonization in the Middle Ages*. Washington, 1917.
— *Feudal Germany*. Chicago, 1928; repr. New York, 1962.
— *The Literacy of the Laity in the Middle Ages*. New York, 1963.
TOECHE, TH. *Kaiser Heinrich VI*. Darmstadt, 1968.
VINOGRADOFF, SIR P. *Roman Law in Medieval Europe*. London/New York, 1909.
WAAS, A. *Herrschaft und Staat im Frühmittelalter*. Berlin, 1938.
— *Der Mensch im deutschen Mittelalter*. Graz/Cologne, 1964.
WADDELL, H. *The Wandering Scholars*. Glasgow/Boston, 1927, New York, 1949.
WALSHE, M. O'C. *Medieval German Literature*. Harvard, 1962.
WATTENBACH, W. AND LEVISON, L. *Deutschlands Geschichtsquellen im Mittelalter. Vorzeit und Karolinger*. Weimar, 1952/57.
WATTENBACH, W. AND HOLTZMANN, R. *Deutschlands Geschichtsquellen im Mittelalter*. I. Das Zeitalter des Ottonischen Staates 900–1050. II. Das Zeitalter des Investiturstreits 1015–1125. Darmstadt, 1967.
WEIGAND, H. J. *Three Chapters on Courtly Love in Arthurian France and Germany*. Chapel Hill, 1956.
WENTZLAFF-EGGEBERT, F. W. *Kreuzzugsdichtung des Mittelalters*. Berlin, 1960.
WHITE, LYNN, JR. *Medieval Technology and Social Change*. Oxford, 1962.
WINSTON, R. *Charlemagne*. New York, 1960.
WOLF, G. ed. *Stupor Mundi. Zur Geschichte Kaiser Friedrichs II von Hohenstaufen*. Darmstadt, 1966.
WORRINGER, W. *Form in Gothic*. New York, 1927.
WULF, M. DE. *Philosophy and Civilization in the Middle Ages*. Princeton, 1922.
— *Histoire de la Philosophie Médiévale*. Paris, 1952.

Sources of Illustrations

Precise references to sources are to be found in the notes on the plates. Acknowledgment for photographs used in the plates is made to the following:

Universitätsbibliothek, Jena, 1; Casa Editrice, Pantheon, Florence, 2, 8, 12, 25, 26, 27, 30; Staatsbibliothek, Munich, 3; Bibliothèque Nationale, Paris, 4; Walter de Gruyter & Co., Berlin, 5, 6, 10, 11, 22, 28, 29; Stadt und Universitätsbibliothek, Frankfurt a. Main, 7a; Syndics of the Fitzwilliam Museum, Cambridge, 7b; Karl Robert Langewiesche Nachfolger Hans Köstler, Königstein im Taunus, 9, 36, 37, 39, 40, 41, 42, 43; Josef Habbel Verlag, Regensburg, 13; Deutscher Verlag für Kunstwissenschaft, Berlin, 14, 31; F. Bruckmann Verlag, Munich, 15; Bildarchiv Foto Marburg, Marburg/Lahn, 16, 17, 19a, 21, 23, 24, 33, 34, 49, 52, 55; Herr Bernt Karger-Decker, Berlin-Weissensee, 18; Klinkhardt & Biermann, Braunschweig, 19b; Kestner Museum, Hanover, 20; Verlag Herder, Freiburg, 32; Frau Helga Schmidt-Glassner, Stuttgart, 35, 53; Kunsthistorisches Museum, Vienna, 38; Photographie Giraudon, Paris, 44; Museum für Kunsthandwerk, Frankfurt a. Main, 45; Woldemar Klein Verlag, Baden-Baden, 46, 47, 48; Frankfurter Verlagsanstalt, Frankfurt a. Main, 50; Ehem. Staatliche Bildstelle, Munich, 51; Frau Lucinde Sternberg-Worringer, Munich, 54; Editions Alpina, Paris (photographs by Jean Roubier, Paris) 56, 57; The Cloisters Collection, Purchase 1947, 58, 59, 60.

1

2

OMNIA QVAE PRAESENS TELLVS PROFVNDA[...]
ET MARIS HAEC FACIES LIMBO CIRCVMINIT[...]
AGNI DM SOLIO TEMET VENERANS VI[...]
CANA CATERVA CLVENS VOTVM PETENTI[...]
COETVS APOSTOLICVS STAT SIC ACIES C[...]
LAVDAT ADORAT AMAT DEVOTO PECTORE [...]
ET PRINCEPS KAROLVS VVLTV SPECVLATVR [...]
ORANS VT TECVM VIVAT LONGE V[...]

4

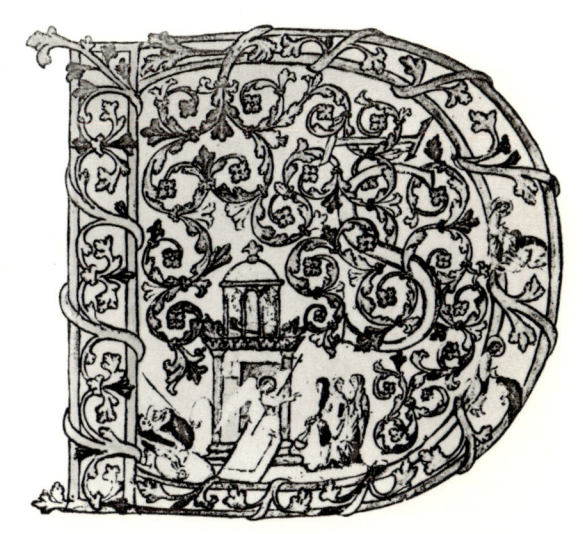

5 6

7 a b

In posteriori genu.
In propoda claram unam
summa xviii. Videntur
& aliae iuxta caudam eius
stellae obscurae .viii.

singulces. In summitate
manus duas. In sinistre
manu duas qui uocantur
haedi. summa.
viiii.

Tauruf haeb& stelles in utro
q; cornu .i. In utroque
oculo .i. In naso .i. hae quin
q; hyades appellentur.
In ungulae .iiii. In collo .ii.
In dorso .ii. ultimam cla
rem. sub uentre unam.
In p&tore unam claram
summa xv.   Sunt &sep
                tē stellę   quae ath
                lantider u̅   piadas
                uocant. que rum sex
uidentur sep ma obscura
est dicuntur que in cauda
tauri positae.

Auriga uel agitator que me
picthonam dicunt. haeb&
stellam in capite .v. In singulis
umeris singulas. In sinistro
claxorem quae appellatur
capra. In singulis genibus

9

10

LXVII DEFECERUNT   LAUDESDDFILIIES   SEPSALMUSASAPh
LIABONUSISRA   LABUNTUR   I DEOCONUERTETURPO
HELDS HISQUIRECTO   I DEOTENUITEOSSUPER   PULUSMEUSHIC EIDIES
SUNTCORDE   BIA OPERTISUNTINI   PLENIINUENIENTUR

11
12
13
14

15

17

16

18

19 a

b

20

21

ftatim occurrit de monumentis homo in spiritu im
mundo. qui domicilium habebat in monumentis
et neque catenis iam quisquam potent ligare. quia
sepe compedib; et catenis uinctus dirupisset eas

22

23

24

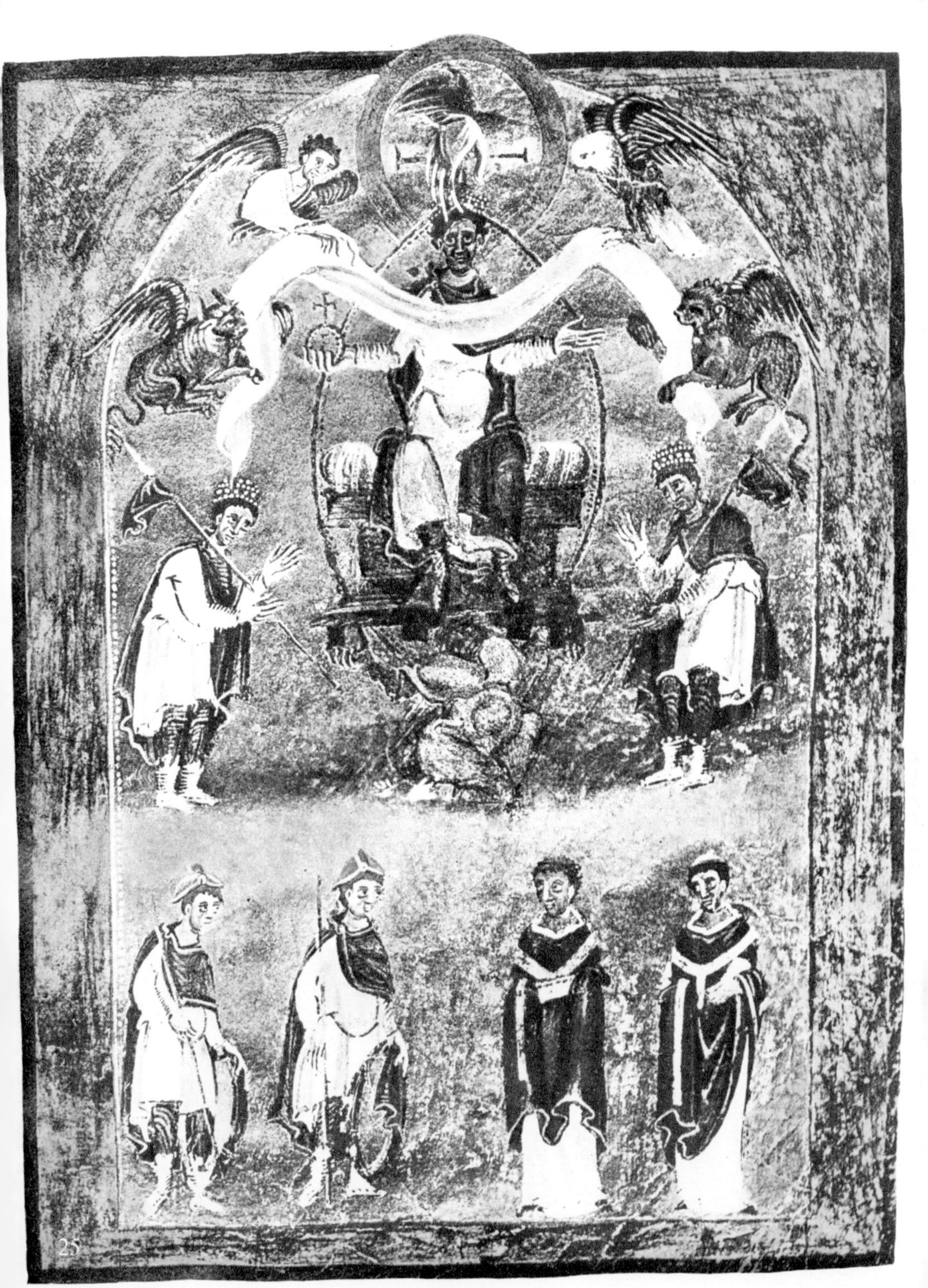

25

26

27

28

29

30

31

32

33

34

35

36

37

38

39 40

41 42

43

44

45

46

47

48

49

50

51

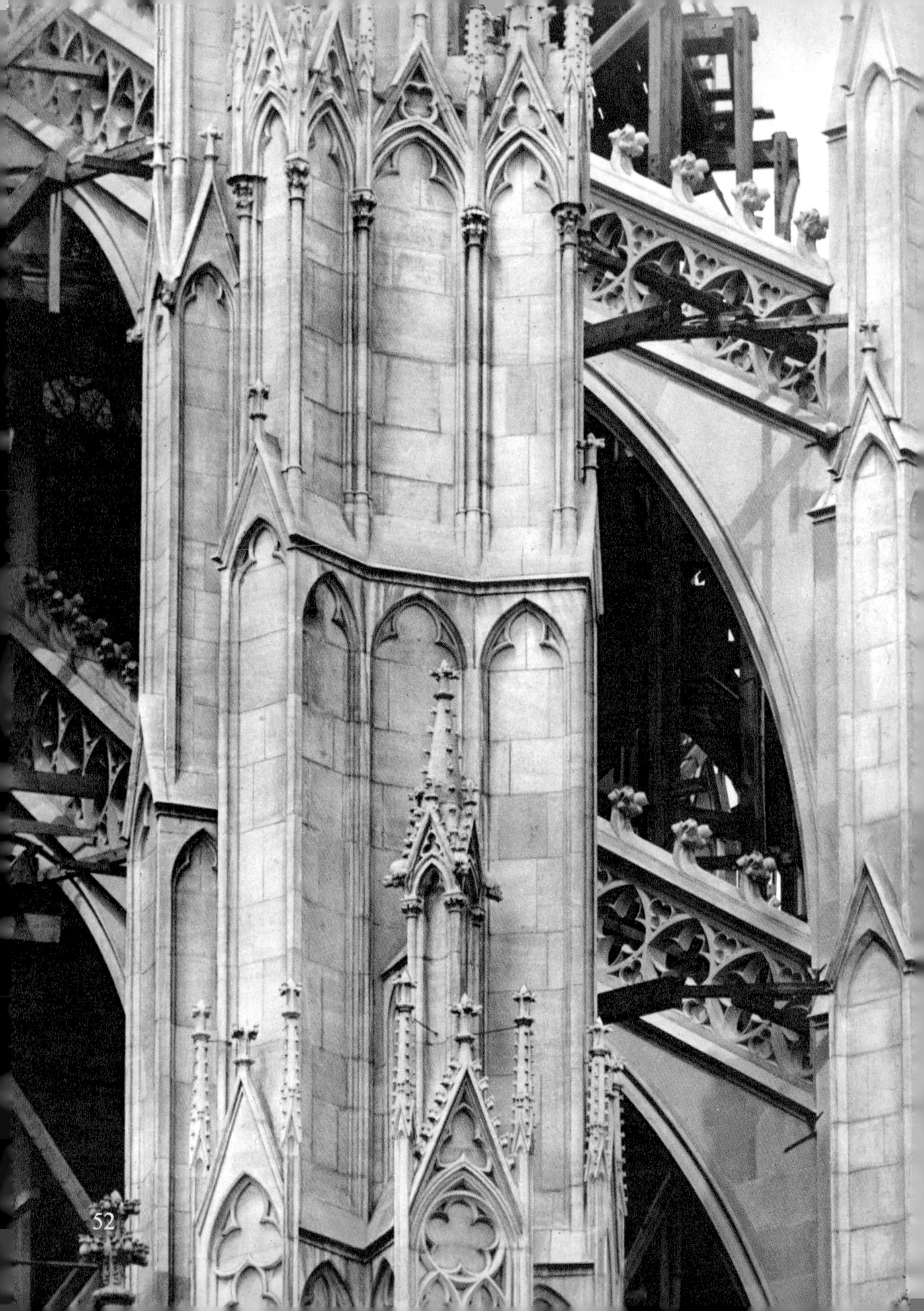

53

54

55

56

57

58

59

60

Notes on the Plates

1 Charlemagne enthroned. The emperor is depicted in the posture traditional for representations of medieval rulers (see Plates 4, 12, 25, 27). Chronicle of Otto of Freising, c. 1157. Codex Jenensis Bose q.6, Universitätsbibl., Jena. (Otto Bischof von Freising, *Chronik oder die Geschichte der zwei Staaten,* plate 10, Berlin 1960.)

2 Dedicatory page of Hrabanus Maurus' *De Laudibus Sanctae Crucis,* showing the author presenting his book to Pope Gregory IV. Rome, Vaticana, Reg. lat. 124. Fulda, second quarter of the ninth century. (A. Goldschmidt, *German Illumination,* I, plate 55b, Florence 1928.)

3 Elders of the Apocalypse. In spite of the two-dimensional and formal treatment, the artist has succeeded in imbuing the scene with an emotional intensity which is heightened by the reiterated ecstatic gesture of the Elders. Codex Aureus from St Emmeram. Bayr. Staatsbibl., Munich. (Kurt Pfister, *Mittelalterliche Buchmalerei des Abendlandes,* plate 20, Munich 1922.)

4 Emperor Lothar. Mid ninth century. Bibl. Nat., Paris. (R. Hinks, *Carolingian Art,* plate 12, Ann Arbor 1962.)

5 Folchard Psalter, 867–72. St Gallen, Stiftsbibl., Cod. 23. (A. Boeckler, *Abendländische Miniaturen,* plate 29, Berlin and Leipzig 1930.)

6 Drogo Sacramentary. Bibl. Nat., Paris, lat. 9428/Metz. (Boeckler, plate 21.)

7 Ivory diptych. The two panels probably once decorated the covers of a sacramentary. Panel a) depicts a priest before the altar at mass; on panel b) he is shown with his right hand raised in blessing, while his left hand holds a book open at the beginning of the twenty-fourth psalm. School

of Metz, a) in the Stadtbibl., Frankfurt a. M.; b) in the Fitzwilliam Museum, Cambridge. (F. X. Kraus, *Geschichte der christlichen Kunst,* II, p. 18, Freiburg i. Br. 1897.)

8 Constellations of Auriga and Taurus. Astrological compilation. Salzburg 818. Staatsbibl., Munich, Cod. lat. 210, fol. 117^v (Goldschmidt, I, plate 15.)

9 Imperial Chapel, Aachen cathedral. Carolingian. (W. Pinder, *Deutsche Dome des Mittelalters, Blaue Bücher* series, p. 21, Königstein im Taunus 1960.)

10 Utrecht Psalter. Written at Hautvillers, near Rheims, *c.* 832, this most famous of the Carolingian psalters is illustrated throughout by marginal vignettes, drawn in a distinctive style. Universiteitsbibl., Utrecht, Bibl. Cod. 32. (Boeckler, plate 19.)

11 St Luke. Miniature from the Ada Gospels. Stadtbibl., Trier. Cod. 22, *c.* 800 (Boeckler, plate 15.)

12 First page of the *Hildebrandslied.* Fulda, ninth century. (Nadler, I, facing p. 20.)

13 Otto II. Musée Condé, Chantilly, No. 14 of Cat. MSS. Registrum Gregorii. (Goldschmidt, II, plate 8.)

14 Book cover. Probably St Emmeram, 1002–25. School of Regensburg, Staatsbibl., Munich. (F. Steenbock, *Der kirchliche Prachteinband im frühen Mittelalter,* plate 79, Berlin 1965.)

15 Reconstruction of the Imperial Palace at Goslar. (Eberhard Hempel, *Geschichte der deutschen Baukunst,* I, plate 61, Munich 1949.)

16 The Imperial Palace at Goslar in its present state.

17 Gernrode, formerly convent-church of St Cyriacus. (Pinder, p. 5.)

18 Henry IV kneeling before Mathilda of Tuscany and abbot Hugo of

Notes on the Plates

Cluny, at Canossa. From the Vita Mathildis, 1114, Vatican. (H. J. Bartmuss *et al., Deutsche Geschichte,* I, p. 275, Berlin 1965.)

19 a) Bronze doors of St Michael's Hildesheim, now in the cathedral. (Goldschmidt, in Hamann's *Die Deutschen Bronzetüren des frühen Mittelalters,* I, fig. 12, Marburg 1926.) b) Fratricide and malediction of Cain. Detail from door of St Michael's Hildesheim. (H. Beenken, *Romanische Skulptur in Deutschland,* p. 5, Leipzig 1924.)

20 Reliquary. Eleventh century. Landesmuseum, Hanover. (*Kunst des frühen Mittelalters,* plate 23, Berner Kunstmuseum catalogue 1949.)

21 Carolingian bronze doors, Aachen cathedral. (Goldschmidt in Hamann's *Bronzetüren,* I, fig. 1.)

22 Codex Egberti. Reichenau, 977–93. Stadtbibl., Trier, Cod. 24. (Boeckler, plate 20.)

23, 24 Codex Egberti. (Goldschmidt, II, plates 4a, b.)

25 Otto II or III with representatives of the nobility and clergy. Title page of the Aachen Otto Codex, Cathedral Treasury, Aachen. (Goldschmidt, II, plate 1.)

26 Nations of the empire paying homage to the emperor. The depiction of the four subject nations has a literary parallel in a book of Gerbert of Aurillac, dedicated to Otto III: 'Ours, ours is the Roman Empire. Fertile Italy, warlike Gaul and Germany render us power, and we also possess the powerful realm of Skythia.' Staatsbibl., Munich. (Goldschmidt, II, plate 24.)

27 Emperor Otto III, Staatsbibl., Munich. (Goldschmidt, II, plate 24.)

28 Codex Aureus. Echternach. 983–92. Landesbibl., Gotha. (Boeckler, plate 33.)

29 Sacramentary. Fulda. *c.* 975. Universitätsbibl., Göttingen, theol. fol. 231. (Boeckler, plate 36.)

30 Codex Aureus. Echternach. 983–92. Landesbibl., Gotha. (Goldschmidt, II, plate 43.)

31 Book cover. Bernward Gospel. End of tenth century. Cathedral Treasury, Hildesheim. (Steenbock, plate 93.)

32 Ceiling decoration in St Michael's, Hildesheim. (Kraus, II, p. 224.)

33 Carved doors. Romanesque. Sta Maria im Kapitol, Cologne. (Paul Clemen, *Die Kunstdenkmäler der Stadt Köln*, p. 234, plate 21, Düsseldorf 1911.)

34 Apostles and prophets. Although they are stylized and exhibit all the characteristics of Romanesque sculpture, these figures are unusually expressive in mien and gesture. Bamberg cathedral, N-side, c. 1230–40. Late Romanesque.

35 Nave, Speyer cathedral.

36, 37 Gospel. Abdinghof. School of Cologne, c. 1070–80. Kupferstichkabinett d. ehem. Staatl. Museen, Berlin-Dahlem, MS. 78 A3. (A. Boeckler, *Deutsche Buchmalerei Vorgotischer Zeit*, pp. 38, 39, Blaue Bücher series, Königstein im Taunus 1959.)

38 Imperial crown. Ottonian. Schatzkammer, Vienna. (Bartmuss, *et al.*, p. 195.)

39 Scene from a Life of St Gertrude. Hirsau. 1110–20. Landesbibl., Stuttgart, Bibl. fol. 57. (Boeckler, *Deutsche Buchmalerei*, p. 42.)

40 Sapientia at the Creation surrounded by Old Testament prophets. Missal from St Michael's, Hildesheim, third quarter of the twelfth century. Reichsfreiherr Kaspar v. Fürstenberg, Brabecke bei Bestwig. (Boeckler, *Deutsche Buchmalerei*, p. 53.)

41 Birth of Christ. Salzburg. Third quarter of the twelfth century. Nationalbibl., Vienna. (Boeckler, *Deutsche Buchmalerei*, p. 45.)

Notes on the Plates

42 Synagoga. Moses in the breast, Abraham in the heart, the prophets in the womb. Hildgard von Bingen, *Liber Scivias*. Middle-Rhenish, third quarter of the twelfth century. Formerly Stadtbibl., Wiesbaden, Cod. I, but lost since the Second World War. (Boeckler, *Deutsche Buchmalerei*, p. 50.)

43 St Paul and his correspondents. Halberstadt. 1175–1200. Universitätsbibl., Tübingen, Depot d. ehem. Preuss. Staatsbibl., theol. lat. fol. 192. (Boeckler, *Deutsche Buchmalerei*, p. 52.)

44 Emperor Frederick Barbarossa as a crusader. Vatican. (J. Le Goff, *La Civilisation de l'Occident médiéval*, plate 24, Paris 1964.)

45 Enamelled box. Swabian? Twelfth century. (*Kunst des frühen Mittelalters*, plate 29, Berner Kunstmuseum catalogue 1949.)

46–48 Emperor Conradin, the margrave of Brandenburg and Walther von der Vogelweide. Manesse MS., Heidelberg. (*Minnesänger*, Baden-Baden 1953.)

49 Ecclesia. Herrad von Landsperg, *Hortus deliciarum*, 1159–75.

50 Archbishop Sifrid of Mainz with Henry Raspe and William of Holland. Tomb of the archbishop, Mainz. (Rudolf Kautzsch, *Der Mainzer Dom und seine Denkmäler*, I, plate 52, Frankfurt 1925.)

51 Vaulting at the crossing, Liebfrauenkirche, Trier. (W. Worringer, *Formprobleme der Gotik*, p. 74, Munich 1911.)

52 Buttresses of Cologne cathedral.

53 Nave of Cologne cathedral.

54 St Quirin's, Neuss. Influence of Gothic is already noticeable in the use of the pointed arch. Late Romanesque. (Worringer, p. 30.)

55 Tympanum, south portal, Strassburg cathedral. (Otto Schmitt, *Gotische Skulpturen des Strassburger Münsters*, I, plate 11, Frankfurt 1924.)

Medieval Civilization in Germany

56, 57 Ecclesia and Synagoga, south portal, Strassburg cathedral. (F. Gebelin, *La Cathédral de Strasbourg,* plates 2 and 3, Paris 1939.)

58 Bronze aquamanile representing a dragon swallowing a monk. Twelfth or thirteenth century. An inventory of the treasury of Mainz cathedral, *c.* 1150, mentions 'ewers of various shapes, called *manilia,* because water is poured from them on the hands of priests.' Their exact purpose is not known. (Metropolitan Museum of Art, New York, Cloisters Collection Purchase 1947.)

59 Chalice made for the abbey of St Trudpert, 1125–1250. On the base are four Old Testament scenes which prefigure the four New Testament scenes on the knob above. The figures of Christ and the apostles surrounding the bowl originated in the seventeenth or eighteenth century, but are probably copies of the original decorations. (Metropolitan Museum of Art, New York, Cloisters Collection Purchase 1947.)

60 Flabellum or liturgical fan of gilded bronze, gold, silver-gilt filigree, tin, enamel and jewels, *c.* 1200. The shape was suggested by the round fans of parchment and feathers which were used to keep flies from the chalice during mass. This flabellum probably served a predominantly ceremonial function and may have been carried in processions with the cross. Usually flabella were carried in pairs. The companion piece of this flabellum is in the Hermitage at Leningrad. (Metropolitan Museum of Art, New York, Cloisters Collection Purchase 1947.)

Index

Aachen 147; imperial chapel at 35, 45, 67, 70
Abelard 19, 20, 106
Absalom of Springiersbach 80
Acre 98
Adalbert of Mainz, archbishop 65
Adam of Bremen 105
Adolf III, count of Holstein 98
'adventure' 132, 135
Aelfric 18
Aeneid 41, 130
Alberic of Besançon 84
Albertus Magnus 113, 114
Albigensian wars 21
Albrecht the Bear 95
Alcuin 26, 27, 28, 29, 30, 40
Alemanni 15
Alexander III, Pope 92, 94
Alexander the Great 84
Alexanderlied 20, 84
Alfonso X, king of Castile 147
Alfred, King 16
allegory 131
Amiens, cathedral of 111, 112
Ancona 101
Andreas Capellanus 20, 125
Angilbert, archbishop of Lyons 29
Anno, archbishop of Cologne 83
Annolied 19, 83
Anselm of Canterbury 19
Apulia 98, 101, 102
Arabic lyric 120
arch, pointed 108

Archipoeta 121
Aristotle 81, 106, 112, 113, 114
Arnulf of Bavaria 17, 44
Arnulf of Carinthia, *see* Arnulf of Bavaria
artes liberales 106
Athelstan 17
Aucassin et Nicolette 21
Augsburg 153
Aurillac, abbey of 67
Austria 119, 121, 122; Duchy of 20; duke of 101
Avars 16
'Averroism' 113
Avicenna 18

Babenberg, dukes of Austria 92
Baltic 150
Bamberg, cathedral of 76, 110
Basle 151
Bavaria 45, 48, 54, 94, 95; duke of 101, 102
Bavarian school of manuscript illumination 78
Beatrice of Burgundy 91
Bede 15, 26, 30, 40
Benedictine monasteries 67
Benevento 22, 148
Bernard of Clairvaux 19
Bernard of San Clemente 88
Bernward, bishop of Hildesheim 69, 70
Berthold of Regensburg 162

223

Besançon, diet of 20, 88
Billung, Hermann 46
Billung, Magnus 54
Boethius 81
Bohemia 100; king of 147, 150
Bouvines, battle of 21, 101
Brandenburg 46, 47; bishop of 103; conquest of 17; duke of 147, 150
Bruno, *Bellum Saxonicum* 105
Burgundy 18, 48, 92
Burkhard of Swabia 44
buttresses 108
Byzantine influence 68, 77, 78

Caedmon 38
Calabria 101
Calixtus II, Pope 64
Cambridge Songs 81, 82
canonical election 56, 64, 101
Canossa 19, 60
Canute 18
Canterbury cathedral 19
Capet, Hugh 18
capitals, Romanesque 68–69
Capitula missorum 23
Capitularia legibus addenda 24
Carmina Burana 121
Carolingian architecture 35, 67; art 33–35, 67, 68, 71, 72, 78, 169
cathedral schools 85, 86
Celestinus III, Pope 98
Chanson de Roland 119
Charles, count of Anjou 148
Charles Martel 33
Charles the Bald 24
Charles III (the Fat) 17, 48

Charles the Great 16, 23, 24, 27, 28, 29, 45, 48, 85, 91
Chartres 29
chivalry 104, 132
Chrétien de Troyes 20, 130, 140
Cistercian architecture 110
Clement III, anti-Pope 61, 62
Clement IV, Pope 148
Clovis 15
Cluniac reform 57, 58, 82, 83, 84, 171
Cluny 17, 57, 58, 67, 76
Codex Aureus, St Emmeram 34
Codex Egberti 18, 70, 71
collections of poetry 163
Cologne 113, 151, 152, 153; archbishop of 100, 147, 150; cathedral of 110; merchants of 150
commerce, revival of 50–51
Confoederatio cum principibus ecclesiasticis 21, 102
Conrad I 17, 44
Conrad II 18, 49, 52, 53, 82
Conrad III 20, 66, 85, 88, 105
Conrad IV 22, 102, 103, 147
Conradin 22, 147, 149
Conrad of Würzburg 158, 159
Constance, peace of 21, 93
Constantine, Emperor 85
Corbie, workshops of 67
Cotrone 18, 49
Crescentia, legend of 85
Crown, imperial 74
Crusade, First 19; Second 20; Third 21, 96

De arte venandi cum avibus 101, 124
De gestis Oddonis I 81

Index

De Heinrico 81
De Sacramentis 86
Denys the Areopagite 30, 31
Deutschenspiegel 106
dialectics 85, 86
Diatessaron 169
Dictatus papae 55–56, 86
Dietmar von Aist 20
Dietrich of Vrieberg 114
Dominican order 20, 113
Drogo of Metz, sacramentary of 34
Duns Scotus Erigena 30, 31, 78
Dürnstein 98

Ecbasis captivi 80
Eckbert of Meissen 61
Eckehart I of St Gallen 80
Eckhart 162
Egbert, archbishop of Trier 71
Eger, Golden Bull of 102
Eike of Repgow 106
Einhard 26, 29
Eneit 20, 130
epic, courtly 130, 131, 159
epic poetry 115, 117
Erec 21, 130, 132, 137, 138
Essen 67
Estonia 103
Ethelred II, King of England 18, 150
Evangelienbuch 169
export 154
Ezzolied 18, 83

Falcon Song 122–126, 172
feudalism 31–33, 65, 88, 92, 95, 106, 153, 156
feudal law 125

Flanders 153
Flarchheim, battle of 61
Franciscan order 113
Frankfurt 147, 153
Frederick I, duke of Swabia 61
Frederick II, duke of Swabia 19, 65
Frederick V, duke of Swabia 97
Frederick I (Barbarossa) 20, 88, 89, 91, 92, 93, 94, 95, 96, 97, 98, 104, 105
Frederick II 21, 22, 99, 101, 102, 103, 124, 147, 153
Freidank 158
Freising 78
Friedrich of Sunnenburg 159
Frisia 63, 147
Froumund 81
Fulda 29, 30, 67, 98

Galicia 104
Gelasius II, Pope 64
Geoffrey of Monmouth 19
Gerbert of Aurillac 17
Gerhard, Der gute 21, 159
Gerhard, master of Cologne cathedral 110–111
Gernrode 68
Gero, margrave 46, 68
Gesta Hammaburgensis 105
gnomic verse 128
Goslar 53, 94
Gothic architecture 106, 107, 108, 109, 110, 112, 171; art 106, 114, 128; sculpture 111
Gottfried of Strassburg 21, 132, 139–140
gradualism 31, 169
Gregory of Tours 24

225

Gregory VII, Pope 19, 55, 57, 58, 60, 61, 64
Gregory VIII, anti-Pope 64
Gregory X, Pope 156
groin-vault 108
Guido of Arezzo 80
Guido of Lusignan 98
guilds 153

Hadrian IV, Pope 104
Halberstadt, bishop of 64
Hanseatic League 103, 150, 151, 153
Hartmann of Aue 130, 132, 137
Hastings, battle of 18
Havelberg 46
Heliant 16, 38, 40
Heinrich of Melk 84
Heinrich of Veldeke 20, 121, 130
Henry V, count palatine 100
Henry the Lion, duke of Saxony and Bavaria 92, 94, 95, 98, 99, 119
Henry the Proud, duke of Saxony and Bavaria 20, 66
Henry, son of Henry the Lion 98
Henry I 17, 44, 46, 48
Henry II, king of England 94
Henry II 18, 49, 52, 150
Henry III 18, 49, 52, 53, 82, 83
Henry III, king of England 147
Henry IV 18, 19, 53, 54, 55, 58, 60, 61, 62, 83, 85, 105
Henry V 19, 62, 63, 64, 65
Henry VI 21, 97, 98, 99, 101
Henry VII 102
Hermann of Luxemburg 61
Hermann of Reichenau 105

Hildebrandslied 16, 36–37
Hildesheim, abbey 67
Hirsau 58, 76, 84
Hohen-Mölsen, battle of 61
Hohenstaufen 66, 91, 99, 101, 103, 146, 149, 164
Hoier of Mansfeld 63
Homburg, battle of 19, 55
horse-collar 42
Hrabanus Maurus 30, 40
Hugh Ripelin 114
Hugh of Strassburg 114
Hugh of St Victor 86, 109

initials, treatment of 34–35
Innocent II, Pope 66
Innocent III, Pope 99, 100
Innocent IV, Pope 148
Interregnum 22, 151, 154, 156, 159, 164
Investiture Contest 56, 62, 64, 78, 82, 83, 86, 91
Isidore of Seville 30
Italy 45, 48, 77, 149
Iwein 21, 130, 132–137, 138

Jagello, king of Poland 103
Jean Bodel 21
Jerusalem 19, 21, 22, 97
John, king of England 21, 101
John the Scot, *see* Duns Scotus Erigena

Kaiserchronik 84
knighthood 119, 120

Index

König Rother 20, 117
Königslutter, abbey church 76
Kudrun 22, 159, 161
Kürenberger, Der 20, 122, 125, 172
Kurland 103

labour, division of 42, 154, 170
Lampert of Hersfeld 105
Lancelot 21
Landesstadt 152
Lechfeld, battle of 18, 46
Legnano, battle of 93, 94
Leopold, duke of Austria 21, 98
Liber Evangeliorum 40
Liège 67
light, tectonic function of 109
Limburg, abbey of 74
Liutprand of Cremona 81
Livland 103
Lombard League 93
Lombardy 67, 91, 92, 94
Lorraine 44, 48, 54, 63
Lothar, Emperor 24, 34, 48
Lothar of Supplinburg, duke of Saxony 19, 65, 66
Louis the Child 17, 44
Louis the German 24
Louis the Pious 16, 24, 38
Louis III 41
Louis IX, king of France 148
love, courtly 125, 127, 128, 130
love lyric, courtly 120, 121, 122, 126, 127, 128, 130, 131, 158, 159, 163
Luceria 103
Lucius III, Pope 83
Lucrece 85

Ludwig the Bavarian 151
Ludwigslied 41
Lübeck 98, 150, 153

Magdeburg 18, 47, 68, 103, 110
Magyars 17, 18, 44, 46, 67, 74
Mainz 60, 101, 150, 153; archbishop of 101, 147, 150; cathedral of 110
Manegold of Lautenbach 86
Manesse manuscript 128
Manfred, king of Sicily 22, 147
Marie de France 20
mariolatry 106
Marner, The 159
Marriage of Mercury and Philology 81
Martianus Capella 81
Mathilda, countess of Tuscany 64, 66, 101
Maximus the Confessor 30
Mechthild of Magdeburg 162
Meier Helmbrecht 161
Meissen 46
Melrichstadt, battle of 61
memento mori 84
Merseburg charms 36
Mersen, treaty of 17
Messina 99
Middle Kingdom 48
Milan 20, 92
mining 154
ministeriales 49, 52, 53, 54, 55, 63, 65, 101, 105, 119, 149, 163
minne, see love, courtly
Minnesang, see love lyric, courtly
modi 82
Modus Ottinc 81

227

monastery schools 85, 86
Moses Maimonides 113
Muspilli 41

Naples 98, 149
narrative art 33-34
Naumburg, cathedral of 110
Neidhart of Reuenthal 128, 156
neoplatonism 30, 114
Nibelungenlied 21, 141-146, 159, 161, 173, 174
Noggerus 84
nominalism 106, 171
Norsemen 67, 74
Notker Balbulus 81, 170
Notker Labeo 18, 81
Notre-Dame de la Basse Oeuvre, Beauvais 74
Notre-Dame, Paris 20
Nuremberg 101, 154

Odo of Metz 35
Odoacer 15
Orendel 118
Otfrid of Weissenburg 17, 30, 40, 169
Otloh of St Emmeram 80, 86
Ottmarsheim 67
Otto-Codex, Aachen 71, 72
Otto of Brunswich (*see* also Otto IV) 100
Otto of Freising 105, 106
Otto of Nordheim 54, 55
Otto of Wittelsbach 95, 100
Otto I 18, 45, 46, 47, 48, 49, 52, 81
Otto II 18, 49, 77
Otto III 18, 49, 53, 72; Gospel of 72
Otto IV 21, 101, 102

Ottokar I, king of Bohemia 101
Ottokar IV, duke of Styria 95
Ottonian art 68, 70, 71, 78, 80
Ovid 120

Padua 113
Paris, university of 106, 113
Parzival 21, 132, 137-138
Paschal II, Pope 63, 64
patriciate 152, 153
Paul the Deacon 29
Peter of Pisa 29
Philip of Heinsberg, archbishop of Cologne 95
Philip Augustus, king of France 21, 97, 98, 100, 101
Philip of Swabia 21, 99, 100
Pipin the Great 15, 33
Plato 114
Poitou 101
Provençal lyric 122, 126
Provence 48, 120
Prüfening 77
Pseudo-Dionysius 78, 80

Quadrivium 26

Rahewîn 105
Rammelsberg silver mines 53, 154
Raspe, Heinrich, landgrave of Thuringia 102
realism 171
Regen, battle on the 62
Regensburg 67, 77, 113
Reichsfürsten 95
Reichenau 29, 67, 70, 71, 72
Reichsstadt 152

Index

Reinmar of Hagenau 21, 126
Reinald of Dassel 88
Rheims 29, 64
Rhenish city league 150, 151
rib-vault 108
Richard, earl of Cornwall 147
Richard I, king of England 21, 97, 98, 99, 100
Roger II, king of Sicily 19
Roland of San Marco 88
Rolandslied 20, 119, 158
Roman d'Eneas 130
Roman de la Rose 22
Romanesque aesthetics 80; architecture 77, 107, 108, 109, 110; art 67, 72, 74, 76, 77–79, 80, 111, 128
Rome, senate of 90
Roncaglia, diet of 20
Roncesvalles 16
roofs, timber 74–75
Roscellinus 106
Roswitha of Gandersheim 80
Rudolf of Ems 21, 159
Rudolf of Habsburg 22, 156, 164
Rudolf of Rheinfelden 60, 61, 105
Ruodlieb 82

Sachsenspiegel 106
St Augustine 40, 84, 85, 105, 113, 114
St Bernard of Clairvaux 86
St Bonaventure 113
St Denis 112
St Denis, workshops of 67
St Etienne cathedral 67
St Francis of Assisi 21
St Martin, Tours 29
St Martin des Champs, abbey of 67
St Martin du Canigou 74
St Michael's, Hildesheim 69, 70, 74
St Oswald 118
St Thomas Aquinas 22, 113, 114, 115
Sta Maria im Kapitol, Cologne 76
Salman and Morolf 118
Saxon dynasty 72, 150; policies of 49
Saxons 16, 38, 47, 54, 55, 105
Saxony 55, 63, 91, 94, 95, 98; duke of 147, 150
Schwabenspiegel 106
Scurcola, battle of 149
sequence 81
Seuse, Heinrich 162
Sic et Non method 112
Sicily 92, 97, 99, 101, 102, 103, 147, 148, 164
Slavs 18, 46, 47, 103, 104
spacial representation 33–34
Speyer 18, 76, 153
Spielmannsepen 115, 117
Spoleto 101
Statutum in favorem principum 22, 102
Steinmar of Klingenau 158
stirrup, introduction of 31–33, 169
Strabo, Walafrid 30
Strassburg 153; cathedral of 110, 111
Strassburg Oaths 16, 24
Stricker, Der 158, 159
Styria 95, 158
Suger, abbot of St Denis 20, 106
summae 86, 112
Swabia 45, 48, 54, 91
Swabian city league 151
Sylvester, Pope 85
symbolism 33, 131, 172; Gothic 109, 110

229

Tagelied 158, 174
Tancred of Sicily 98
Tatian 169
Tauler, Johannes 162
Teutonic Knights 103
Theodulf, bishop of Orléans 29
Theophano, princess 77
Thomas á Becket 20
Thomas of Brittany (Britain) 140
three-field cultivation 43
Thuringia 46, 47, 55, 63
Thuringians 15, 54
Tours, workshops of 67
Tribur, diet of 60
Trier, archbishop of 147, 150
Tristan and Isolt 132, 139–141
trivium 26, 81
Tugumir 47
Tuscany 93, 94
two-field cultivation 42

Ulrich Engelbrecht 114
Ulrich of Strassburg 114
Ulrich of Liechtenstein 156, 158, 159
uncial, Carolingian 28
Urban II, Pope 62
Urban IV, Pope 148
urbanization 152

vagantes 121
vaulting 75, 76
Venice, Peace of 21
Verdun, Treaty of 16, 24
Victimae paschalis 82
Vulgate 40

Wace 20
Waltharius manu fortis 40, 80
Walther von der Vogelweide 20, 22, 127, 128, 129, 146
Welfesholz, battle of 63, 65
Welfs 67, 98, 150
Wendish crusade 20
Werner der Gärtner 161
Westphalia 63, 95
Widukind of Corvey 81
William of Champeaux 106
William of Holland 102–3, 147
William the Conqueror 19
William II, king of Sicily 97
windows, stained glass 108, 109
Wipo 82
Witelo 109
Wittelsbach, dynasty of 92, 150
Wolfram of Eschenbach 21, 132, 137
Worms, cathedral of 110; Concordat of 19, 64, 66; Synod of 19

Zähringen, dynasty of 92